HOW TO THINK STRAIGHT

HOW TO THINK STRAIGHT

An Introduction to Critical Reasoning

ANTONY FLEW

Prometheus Books

59 John Glenn Drive
Amherst, New York 14228-2197

Published 1998 by Prometheus Books

How to Think Straight: An Introduction to Critical Reasoning. Copyright © 1998 by Antony Flew. All rights reserved. No part of this publication may be reproduced, stored in a retrieval system, or transmitted in any form or by any means, digital, electronic, mechanical, photocopying, recording, or otherwise, or conveyed via the Internet or a Web site without prior written permission of the publisher, except in the case of brief quotations embodied in critical articles and reviews.

Inquiries should be addressed to
Prometheus Books
59 John Glenn Drive
Amherst, New York 14228–2197
VOICE: 716–691–0133, ext. 207
FAX: 716–564–2711
WWW.PROMETHEUSBOOKS.COM

06 05 04 03 02   8 7 6 5 4

Library of Congress Cataloging-in-Publication Data

Flew, Antony.
　　[Thinking about thinking]
　　How to think straight : an introduction to critical reasoning / by Antony Flew.
　　　　p.　　cm.
　　Originally published: Thinking about thinking.
　　Includes bibliographical references and index.
　　ISBN 1–57392–239–0 (alk. paper)
　　1. Thought and thinking. I. Title.
BF455.F614　　1998
160—dc21　　　　　　　　　　　　　　　　　　　　　　　　　98–8517
　　　　　　　　　　　　　　　　　　　　　　　　　　　　　　CIP

Printed in the United States of America on acid-free paper

We must follow the argument wherever it leads.

Socrates (Fifth Century B.C.E.)

A man who will not reason about anything is no better than a vegetable.

Aristotle (Fourth Century B.C.E.)

A moment's thought would have shown him. But a moment is a long time, and thought is a painful process.

A. E. Housman (Twentieth Century C.E.)

Many people would sooner die than think—in fact, they do so.

Bertrand Russell (Twentieth Century C.E.)

Contents

Foreword

The present work is a revised and greatly expanded version of a book originally published in the United Kingdom as *Thinking about Thinking* and later reissued in the United States of America as *Thinking Straight*. The revision is primarily an update of the original work. References to controversies since deceased have been replaced by others more topical. But there has also been some simplification, intended to make the contents easier for readers to master. The purpose of the expansion was to introduce additional useful material, especially material relevant to what have become major controversial issues since the appearance of the first edition. Among these are, for instance, controversies about pollution, conservation, and the proportionate representation of various perceived minorities in different areas of activity and achievement.

Among members of the class of books aimed at the improvement of the quality of thinking, *Thinking Straight* was from the beginning distinctive in two ways. One was the frequency of references to the ideas both of various classical philosophers and of other major thinkers such as Karl Marx. I have been told by colleagues who have used *Thinking Straight* as the required text for critical thinking courses that these references have led some of their pupils to sign up for further courses in

9

departments of philosophy. This has encouraged me to introduce into this second edition both paragraph-long quotations from René Descartes and David Hume and other equally relevant, shorter quotations from Thomas Aquinas, John Locke, Thomas Hobbes, and, again, David Hume. I have also introduced parenthetic references to various books with which those seriously engaging in these current controversies need somehow to come to terms. That, as was made very clear in the frequent use of that expression by Karl Marx, is by no means the same as coming to agree!

The second distinctive feature of *Thinking Straight* is indicated by the subtitle given to the first edition. It was: "Or, Do I Sincerely Want to Be Right?" Other books about critical thinking at least tend to suggest to their readers that the authors' chief concern is helping readers protect themselves against deception by unsound arguments urged, whether innocently or intentionally, by other people. Certainly this is necessary work. But it is not sufficient. A prime cause of our being deceived is, for all of us, always our own desire to be so deceived. *How to Think Straight: An Introduction to Critical Reasoning* therefore insists throughout that all of us constantly need to be asking ourselves what it is which we want to believe to be true, and whether our desires so to believe are stronger than our desires to know the truth, however uncongenial to us that truth may be. It is a truly existential challenge.

Antony Flew
26 Alexandra Road
Reading RG1 5PD
England

1

The Basic Equipment

1.1 The first thing to get straight in thinking about thinking is the difference between questions about validity and questions about truth. But in getting this straight we shall find that we are also sorting out every other really fundamental notion. For the indispensable notions are all connected. We cannot fully master any one without getting the same grasp upon the lot. Once the essential preparation is complete, we may proceed to the main business of the book. That business is to consider examples of thinking, usually of bad thinking, in order to learn how to do the job better. Here and now we have first to clean and tidy the tools.

1.2 The reason to begin precisely where we are beginning is that thinking about thinking is concerned, at least in the first instance, with the validity or invalidity of arguments, rather than with the truth or falsity of propositions. What is true, or false, is propositions. What is valid, or invalid, is arguments. These notions and these distinctions are absolutely basic. To say that an argument is true or that a proposition is valid is as uncomprehending or as inept as to say that someone got to first base in basketball or that someone made a home run in tennis.

1.3 Consider propositions. There are, of course, propositions and propositions. Both those mutually advantageous proposals which one businessman makes to another and those improper but delightful suggestions which playboys put to their intended playmates are called, quite properly, "propositions." But in this book—perhaps regrettably— we shall engage with propositions only in a quite different sense of the word. In this, our relevant sense, the word "proposition" is defined as, "whatever may be asserted or denied." So a proposition for us becomes whatever may be expressed by the that-clause in such sentences as, "She asserted that he had been there on Wednesday," or "He denied that he had ever met her."

1.4 In the irrelevant, proposal sense a proposition may be said to be attractive or unattractive, profitable or unprofitable, and many other things besides. What it cannot be, or be said to be, is either valid or invalid. In our different sense there are again several things which a proposition may be: demonstrated, for instance, or probable, or refuted. Nevertheless, the primary characteristic is truth or falsity. For demonstration here is nothing else but proving that the proposition is true. The proposition which is probable just is probably true. Refutation, again, is not merely saying, but showing, that the proposition is false. It is because refutation involves more than denial that hard-pressed spokespersons so often assert that they have refuted charges when in fact all that they have done is deny them, perhaps dishonestly.

1.5 Propositions in this understanding are not to be identified with arguments, although all arguments contain propositions. Piety demands that our first example be a dull hack hallowed by immemorial tradition. Its tedious, trite, and trivial character will ensure that no one is distracted from what is being illustrated by any interest in the illustration. Later I shall deploy interesting and important examples. I hope thus to escape the dangers of boring myself and everybody else, or suggesting that the subject itself is as trifling as this first illustration.

1.6 Set out carefully and piously, the traditional example runs: if *All men are mortal*, and if *Socrates was a man*, then it follows necessarily that *Socrates was mortal*. This example includes three constituent propositions. The first two serve as premises, the last as a conclusion. In other contexts and in other arguments what is here conclusion might serve as premise, and what are here premises might be derived as conclusions from other premises.

1.7 The italicization of the constituent propositions and the representation of the whole argument in a hypothetical (if this, then) form are both important. The first device brings out two things: first, in general, that arguments are concerned with the logical relations between propositions; and second, in particular, what proposition is being said to be necessarily connected with what two others. Later much more will be said both about logical relations and about logically necessary connections. For the moment it is sufficient, but necessary, to emphasize that these are always and only relations of, and connections between, propositions.

1.8 The second of the two devices, that of representing a whole argument in hypothetical form, makes it clear why, in order to know whether the exemplary argument in which these three propositions are here embodied is valid, we do not need to know whether any of its constituent propositions are true. We do not for this purpose need to know because in offering the argument we are not actually saying anything about the truth or falsity of these constituent propositions. It is all hypothetical. Another argument of the same form would be no less valid even if all of its three constituent propositions happened in fact to be false. This would be true of the absurd argument: If *All tigers are strictly vegetarian,* and if *Socrates the son of Sophroniscus was a tiger,* then it follows necessarily that *Socrates the son of Sophroniscus was strictly vegetarian.* As we shall see in chapter 2, such hypothetical deductions, albeit from much more sensible premises, may serve as the initial steps in a more complex pattern of argument. Such deductions lead us from the actual falsity of the original conclusion in a valid argument to the further conclusion that at least one of the original premises must also be false.

1.9 Although to say that the present argument is valid is thus not to say that any of the three constituent propositions are true, it does imply the truth of the complex hypothetical proposition: If *All men are mortal,* and if *Socrates was a man,* then it follows necessarily that *Socrates was mortal.* In asserting this truth, what is asserted is that the argument from the two constituent premise propositions to the constituent conclusion proposition is valid. The fact that you can say that the claim that this argument is valid (or invalid) is a true (or false) claim is, however, no more a justification for confounding validity with truth than the fact that you can say that the contention that a certain man is a homosexual is a true (or false) contention is a warrant for identifying homosexuality with truth.

1.10 To say that an argument is deductively valid is, by definition, to say that it would be impossible to assert its premise or premises while denying its conclusion or conclusions without thereby contradicting oneself. That is what deduction is. We have just seen that an argument may be valid, notwithstanding that both its premise or premises and its conclusion or conclusions are false. Similarly, an argument may be invalid, notwithstanding that both its premise or premises and its conclusion or conclusions are true.

1.11 Later we shall return to the relations and lack of relations between validity and truth, and I will provide mnemonic illustrations. But the first thing now is to underline the connection between the two concepts of deductive validity and of contradiction and to explain what is so wrong about contradiction. Suppose someone were to maintain that, although *Socrates was a man, Socrates was not mortal*. No doubt such apparent irrationality in so simple a case is somewhat hard to imagine. Yet that difficulty should, if anything, make it easier to appreciate that if ever people were to behave in this way, then we would have to choose between two alternative conjectures. Either they are being in some way disingenuous, or else they are not fully masters of the meanings of all the words which they have uttered.

1.12 On the one hand, perhaps they have some sort of doctrinal commitment to affirm the two premises while nevertheless equally firmly denying the obvious conclusion. They may want to maintain that Socrates was a man and, as such, mortal, and yet that Socrates was a god and, as such, not mortal. Certainly there are those who hold that someone, though not Socrates (c. 470–399 B.C.E.), was at the same time both truly man and truly God. Or maybe our imaginary objectors have their reasons for wanting to say one thing in one context or to one group of people while saying something altogether inconsistent in another context or to another group of people. This temptation is familiar to us all. It is no prerogative of members of that scapegoat class, professional politicians.

1.13 On the other hand, it is also possible that our imaginary objectors are careless or confused about the crucial difference between all and some. *Some men are mortal* is consistent, as *All men are mortal* is not, with *Some men are not mortal*. Again, there is no call for any far-fetched supposing. We meet all too many cases of people who, having noticed that something or other is true for a few instances of such and such a sort of thing, proceed forthwith to assume, or even to assert, that the same is true of all things of that sort. We have, surely, all done it ourselves? (Such generalizations about all and every something or other are, by the way, called universal propositions.)

1.14 There may appear to be a third possibility, that an objector might be interpreting one of the key terms in one way in one of the premises and in another way in the other premise or in the conclusion. The word "Socrates," for instance, might be employed to refer to one person on one occasion and to another on the other. Again, "mortal" might be construed as meaning "liable to death," whereas "not mortal" was understood as metaphorically "immortal"—immortal, that is, in that wholly different sense in which a great person who indisputably has died, or will sometime die, may nevertheless truly and consistently be numbered among the immortals.

1.15 This apparent third possibility is thus the possibility of equivocation. The word "equivocation" is here defined as "the employment of some word or expression in two or more different senses without distinction in the same context." If equivocators realize that they are equivocating in their employment of one of the key terms in an argument, then their performances are certainly disingenuous. If they do not realize this, then, equally certainly, they are "not fully masters of the meanings of all the words they have uttered." In the most literal sense they do not know what they are talking about.

1.16 The basic point developed in the five previous paragraphs is extremely important. It is none the less so for having been made with a hackneyed, traditional example developed in a somewhat far-fetched way. This basic point is that the terms "valid" and "invalid," as applied to deductive arguments, and the expression "deductive argument" itself have all to be defined in terms of self-contradiction and the avoidance of self-contradiction. It is because these are thus central notions that our concern with logic inextricably involves us also in concerns with both meaning and truth. The basis of the necessary and inescapable involvement with meaning will be immediately obvious. Given that a valid deductive argument is, by definition, one in which to assert the premises while denying the conclusion is to contradict yourself, then it becomes at once clear that no one can be in a position to know whether or not any argument is valid, except insofar as he or she has mastered the meanings of all its crucial terms.

1.17 It may be more difficult to appreciate that there are necessary connections between logic and truth and why these connections make it so essential to argue validly and to avoid contradiction. For did not this chapter itself begin by insisting that "thinking about thinking is concerned, at least in the first instance, with the validity or invalidity of arguments rather than with the truth or falsity of propositions"? And have we not gone on to assert that arguments may be valid, though both their premises and their conclusions happen to be false, or invalid, though both their premises and their conclusions are in fact true?

1.18 Yes, this was said. It is all true. But it is also true that, though sound argument and a reasonable appreciation of the available evidence may happen sometimes to lead to false conclusions, no man who is indifferent to argument and to evidence can claim to be concerned for truth. Abraham Lincoln was profoundly right when he wrote, chiding the editor of a Springfield, Illinois, newspaper: "It is an established maxim and moral that he who makes an assertion without knowing whether it is true or false is guilty of falsehood, and the accidental truth of the assertion does not justify or excuse him." It is also true that to tolerate contradiction is similarly to be indifferent to truth. For people who, whether directly or by implication, knowingly both assert and deny one and the same proposition show by that behavior that they do not care whether they assert what is false and not true, or whether they deny what is true and not false.

1.19 To grasp this point is to raise a perennial personal challenge. Like all such personal challenges, it should be seen as being at least as much a challenge to me and to us as it is to you and to them. For whenever and wherever I tolerate self-contradiction, then and there I make it evident, either that I do not care at all about truth, or that at any rate I do care about something else more. It was thus precisely because to affirm the premises of a valid deductive argument while denying the conclusion is, by the definition of "valid deductive argument," to contradict yourself, that Socrates used to demand: "We must follow the argument wherever it leads."

1.20 The same personally challenging point, that contradiction must be intolerable to anyone who really cares about truth, can, with the help of a little demonstration, be made more elaborately. Anyone inclined to bridle against such logic-chopping can without serious loss skip the next four paragraphs. The promised, or threatened, demonstration was apparently first mounted in the 1200s of our era either by Duns Scotus (c. 1266–1300) or by one of his pupils. (It is, by the way, ultimately to the uninhibited polemics of the philosophical opponents of the great Duns Scotus that we all owe our word "dunce." There must be some moral here!)

1.21 The demonstration goes like this: First, take as your personal premise a contradiction of your choice. I take for mine the conjunction of the two propositions: (1) *The Declaration of Independence was made in 1776*; and (2) *The Declaration of Independence was not made in 1776*. Now choose, equally freely, any false proposition. I choose: *Elvis Presley is alive and well*. Next, take one half of the initial contradiction as a separate premise. From *The Declaration of Independence was made in 1776* it follows that *The Declaration of Independence was made in 1776* and/or *Elvis Presley is alive and well*.

1.22 Thus, given that for whatever x may be, x *is true*, then for the same value of x and for any value of y it follows necessarily that x *and/or* y *is true*. The only, but sufficient, justification for employing the symbols x and y—rather than the awkward verbal alternatives *something, the same something, something else*, and *the same something else*—is that the point can thereby be made more briefly, more clearly, and more elegantly. The object is, as it always should be, to promote understanding. What needs to be understood is that so far it has been shown that, from my arbitrarily chosen contradictory premise, it follows that *The Declaration of Independence was made in 1776* and/or *Elvis Presley is alive and well*. So far so unexceptionable, and altogether unexciting.

1.23 But now we consider the second half of the initial contradiction: *The Declaration of Independence was not made in 1776.* Taking this as one premise and the conclusion reached at the end of paragraph 1.21 as the other, it becomes impossible to avoid the false conclusion that *Elvis Presley is alive and well.* For to deny this while asserting these two premises would be to contradict oneself.

1.24 We thus have an absolutely general and absolutely compulsive demonstration that from any contradiction which you like to choose, any other proposition, equally arbitrarily chosen, follows necessarily. By the same token, the negation of that other, arbitrarily chosen, proposition must also follow, equally necessarily. We can by the same method also deduce the opposite conclusion: *Elvis Presley is not alive and well.* Both every proposition and its negation thus follows from any contradiction. Hence, if contradiction is tolerated, then, in a very literal sense, anything goes. This situation must itself be totally intolerable to anyone who has any concern at all to know what is in fact true and to avoid either saying or implying what is in fact false. If all this seems pedantic, recall Bertrand Russell's mischievous definition of a pedant: "A person who prefers his statements to be true."

1.25 Generally, therefore, when someone with pretensions to be a thinker either denounces the restrictions of logic or remains unmoved by charges of self-contradiction, we know what to think. Thomas Aquinas (c. 1225–1274) understood as well as any man that the saints and the prophets may speak of mysteries. Yet, having a grip on logical fundamentals, Aquinas never forgot that there can be no place for self-contradiction in any authentic quest for truth. Thus, in considering the omnipotence to be attributed to his God, he took account of what is in modern terms the distinction between logical and other senses of "impossibility." A suggestion is said to be logically impossible if that suggestion contains or implies a self-contradiction, or is perhaps otherwise incoherent and unintelligible. But a suggestion that is not in this sense logically impossible may be ruled out by the actual laws of nature and hence be factually impossible. As Aquinas put it in the *Summa Theologica:* "Whatever does not imply a contradiction is, consequently, among those possibilities in virtue of which God is described as omnipotent. But what does imply a contradiction is not subsumed under the divine omnipotence . . ." (I Q25 A3). You cannot, he might have said, transmute some incoherent mixture of words into sense merely by introducing the three-letter word "God" to be its grammatical subject.

1.26 One place where this distinction and this insight is indispensable is in the discussion of what theists call "The Problem of Evil." This is the theists' problem of trying to show that they are not contradicting themselves in maintaining both that there is, as indeed there is, much evil in the Universe and that the Universe is the work of an all-powerful, all-good God. It is not a bit of use to appeal here to what are, the Universe being as it happens to be, factual impossibilities. The only hope for the theist is to try to show that it would be logically impossible to have the actual goods without the actual evils, as it is, for instance, logically impossible to have the good of forgiveness without the evil of an injury to be forgiven. It is logically impossible because it is self-contradictory to speak of forgiving a nonexistent injury. For the theist it must be almost blasphemous to argue here, along lines I once saw indicated by one of a series of posters described as constituting The Wayside Pulpit: "If it never rained, there would be no hay to make when the sun shone."

1.27 The most fundamental kind of confusion about contradiction is an intellectual malpractice that Karl Marx (1818–1883) and Friedrich Engels (1820–1895) derived from their study of the enormously influential German philosopher G. W. F. Hegel (1770–1831). This is the malpractice of thinking of contradictions not only as occurring in discourse, but also as involved in the interactions of physical objects. Thus, in the essay *On Contradiction* supposedly written by Mao Tse-tung, we can read: "The supersession of the old by the new is the universal, forever inviolable law of the world. . . . Everything contains a contradiction between its new aspect and its old aspect, which constitutes a series of intricate struggles. . . . At the moment when the new aspect has won the dominant position over the old aspect, the quality of the old thing changes into the quality of the new thing. Thus the quality of a thing is mainly determined by the principal aspect of the contradiction that has won the dominant position."

1.28 A contradiction in this regrettable usage is thus not a verbal contradiction, but a conflict or a tension in or between things or people. Once these categories are properly distinguished, the apparent justification for employing the same word in two utterly different cases disappears. To the extent that this usage helps to collapse or to confound a categorical distinction, it is to be deplored. This same usage encourages talk of fruitful or even nonantagonistic contradictions, contradictions that are welcome, or at least venial. (Mao Tse-tung himself continued, speaking of the "contradiction" between town and country: "But in a socialist nation and in our revolutionary bases such an antagonistic contradiction becomes a nonantagonistic contradiction; and it will disappear when a communist society is realized. . . .")

1.29 But talk of fruitful (if not, perhaps, of nonantagonistic) contradictions may have quite a different source. The contradictions then referred to are genuine verbal or symbolic contradictions, and the fruit offered has to be picked by laboring to remove the contradiction. The vital point for us is that this fruitfulness presupposes the removal of the contradiction. It is only insofar as contradiction is recognized to be intolerable that the labors which may provide fruit can begin.

1.30 Consider, for instance, disagreements about whether or not some country is democratically governed. Very obviously the party who asserts that it is appears to be contradicting the party who asserts that it is not. But perhaps these two disputants are employing the key word "democratic" in different senses. For one of them the criteria for a democracy may be that the rulers should have been popularly elected into office and—much more important—that it should be possible in due course to vote them out. For the other one the criterion may be that favored by rulers describing their fiefs as people's democracies, namely, that these rulers are working to promote the best interests of those whom they rule. One by now rather ancient, yet still remarkably clear expression of this conception of democracy was provided by Janos Kadar, addressing the Hungarian National Assembly on May 11, 1957, one year after a Soviet army of intervention had installed him into office as prime minister: "The task of the leaders is not to put into effect the wishes and will of the masses. . . . The task of the leaders is to accomplish the interests of the masses." This statement may profitably be compared and contrasted with that made by Abu Zuhair Yahya, prime minister of Iraq in 1968: "I came in on a tank, and only tanks will get me out" (quoted in Luttwak 1969, p. 146).

1.31 Because of the Hegelian or Hegelian-Marxist confusion involved in speaking of contradictions in things and because salutary challenges to resolve seeming but not actual contradictions may be preposterously misconstrued as reasons for rating actual contradictions as in themselves good, contradiction sometimes wins an undeservedly favorable press. Similar confusions and misunderstandings often get an understandably bad press for logic.

1.32 The first of these misunderstandings hinges on a failure to distinguish two senses of the word "logic." One is primary. It is the sense in which the word has been employed in this chapter up till now. The other is secondary and derivative. This is the sense in which it is true to say that Aristotle (384–322 B.C.E.), in the works grouped into what was later called the *Organon*, created "Logic" as an academic discipline. These two senses are most conveniently distinguished by printing the word with an initial capital whenever it is used in the second sense.

1.33 The general mistake here is that of expecting any study of that kind to be either necessary or sufficient to improve the practice to which it is directed. The musicologist does not through his musicology become a better executant. Nor does being a great performer immediately qualify one to be a musicologist. The particular point about "Logic" and "logic" was made in the late 1600s by John Locke (1632–1704) in his *Essay concerning Human Understanding*: "God has not been so sparing to men to make them barely two-legged creatures, and left it to Aristotle to make them rational; . . ." (IV [xvii] 4).

1.34 On the contrary: "Logic," as the theoretical study of the forms and principles of argument, could only begin among and be pursued by people possessing a good practical capacity to separate valid from invalid arguments. In fact, its first strong and extensive development was among the ancient Greeks and, in particular, among the supremely argumentative Athenians. (For a lively and instructive study of the peculiarities of these Greeks, which made possible the origination of so much that was essential to the development of our modern world, see Alan Cromer's *Uncommon Sense: The Heretical Nature of Science* [1993], especially chapters 4–6.) The present book, which is intended to help people to improve their thinking, is not an essay in theoretical Logic. It is instead an exercise in logical coaching. Such an exercise may be beneficial even though neither the coach nor the coached have or acquire any familiarity with the calculi of Logic. But it could not even begin, much less be beneficial, unless all concerned possessed at least some minimal competence in discerning soundness in argument. Without that you could not even understand the coaching.

1.35 The second and much more important reason why logic gets a bad press is that it is confused with various things which have nothing to do with it. Consider, for instance, the contrast and the possible conflict between two opposite approaches to politics and to society. On the one side are those who, like Plato (c. 428–c. 348 B.C.E.), want, as he put it in his dialogue *The Republic*, "to start with a clean canvas." A good example of this approach was provided by the Jacobins during the great French Revolution of 1789. They replaced all the previous subdivisions of France by eighty-three Departments, all roughly equal in area and each with its own administrative center. They also introduced a new calendar of twelve months with freshly minted names, and all the months were divided into three decads of ten days each. (A special arrangement was made to accommodate the surplus five days.) And so on. On the opposite side are those, like Aristotle, who prefer to start from wherever they are, seeing improvement as a matter of natural growth and development. Reformers of the first kind are likely to long for utopia and to have a penchant for wholesale operations. Reformers of the second kind do not expect anything to be perfect and believe that whatever progress can be made has to be made piecemeal. They understand, with the great German philosopher Immanuel Kant (1724–1804), that "out of the crooked timber of humanity no straight thing can ever be made."

1.36 Especially in the context of thinking about the French Revolution of 1789, the first great social revolution of the modern period, Edmund Burke (1729–1797)* is often seen as representative of the second approach. This approach is sometimes believed by English people to be characteristically English, although Burke himself was

---

*Burke was a member of the U.K. Parliament, most famous for his hostile and horrified *Reflections on the Revolution in France*. (He had been and remained sympathetic to the very different American Revolution.)

born and educated in Ireland. By contrast, the Abbé Sieyès,* who con-
trived to survive when so many of the other revolutionaries were killed,
is seen as representative of the first approach, an approach which is in
the same circles seen as characteristically French. Neither of these
approaches is as such either logical or illogical, although particular
spokespersons on one side or the other may well be logical or illogical.
But when confronted with the argument of the Abbé Sieyès against leg-
islative second chambers, his supporters are apt to applaud his famous
apothegm as a fine specimen of Gallic logic while his opponents decry
it upon exactly the same ground. What he said was: "If the second
chamber agrees with the first, it is superfluous, whereas if it disagrees
with it, it is obnoxious."

1.37 It is not for us here to decide whether this statement is especially Gallic. We do, however, need to notice that it certainly is not especially logical. If someone accepted the two conditional propositions so
dogmatically asserted, then it would, of course, be illogical for that
person to refuse to allow that any second chamber agreeing with the first
must be superfluous and that any second chamber disagreeing with the
first must be obnoxious. Yet there is no intellectual or other merit in
simply asserting these drastic propositions. By doing so you make the
totalitarian assumption, without providing any supporting evidence, that
all dissent from any decision made by the first chamber must be immediately and automatically overridden. This is an assumption which no
one has any business to make tacitly and without supporting argument.
When such a brilliant refusal to examine the case for the opposition is
presented as a model of logic, then there is every excuse to be suspi-
cious. But it is not in this interpretation that we are laboring to make
ourselves more logical.

1.38 We have shown why contradiction ought to be unacceptable
and that logic is connected, albeit indirectly, with truth. It should now
be less misleading to insist again upon the fundamental difference
between questions about validity and questions about truth. To fix this
in mind we need one or two dull, undistracting, naggingly unforgettable

---

*The Abbé Sieyès is most famous for his answer to the question: "What did
you do in the Revolution?" His reply was: "I survived." But one might mention his
pamphlet *What Is the Third Estate?* (1790).

examples. Consider as premises the two propositions: *All philosophers are lifelong bachelors* and *King Henry VIII of England was a philosopher*. Both are false. But if they were true, then it would follow necessarily that *King Henry VIII of England was a lifelong bachelor*. Anyone who asserts the two false premises, yet denies the conclusion, would certainly be committing a self-contradiction. So now, since few people have less claim to have been lifelong bachelors than King Henry VIII, who was married six times, we have an example of a valid argument from false premises to a false conclusion.

1.39 Next, suppose that we substitute for the original second premise: *President James Buchanan was a philosopher*. Then, again, both premises will be false. Tl.e conclusion will be that *President James Buchanan was a lifelong bachelor*. Applying the same test as before, it is obvious that this is derived by a valid deductive argument. But this time the conclusion is true. Thus, we now have an example of a valid argument from false premises to a true conclusion.

1.40 Someone says: *All Christians believe in an omnipotent and personal God*, and *Mother Teresa believed in an omnipotent and personal God*. If we assume that these two propositions are true, are we entitled, taking them as our premises, to deduce the conclusion: *Mother Teresa was a Christian*? No, of course we are not. Certainly the conclusion is true. Yet the argument, considered as an argument, is, equally certainly, invalid. To make it valid, the first premise would have to be changed to read not *All Christians*, but *All and only Christians*. So the example offered, without that essential amendment, constitutes an example of an invalid argument to a conclusion which happens nevertheless to be true.

1.41 Suppose that some people have difficulty in appreciating that such an argument must be invalid, as indeed many people may have since they happen to know that its conclusion is in fact true. Then the natural and appropriate response is to summon up parallels to enable those who have this difficulty to appreciate that neither this nor any other argument of the same form can possibly be sound. You might as well argue, we might say, that given that *All swans are white* (which they are not), and given that *President William Clinton is white* (which, in terms of race, he is), then it follows necessarily that *President William Clinton is a swan* (which will scarcely do). Or, again, you might as well argue that given that *All Communists claimed to be opposed to racism* and given that *Dr. Martin Luther King claimed to be opposed to racism,* then it follows necessarily, *Dr. Martin Luther King was a Communist.*

1.42 When we produce such parallels, we are trying to bring out the invalidity of all arguments of one particular form: the form, that is, and whatever it is, which is shared by both the original specimen and all the genuine parallels which could be deployed. The main practical reasons why parallels have to be summoned is that people are put off by what they know or believe about particular propositions in particular arguments. Because we know or believe that the proposed conclusion is true, we become less alert to the possible weakness of the inference by which it is supposedly derived.

1.43 If, therefore, we want to assess someone else's critical acumen, then the best way to do this is to attend to their responses to arguments apparently justifying the conclusions which are most congenial to them. And when, as we should do frequently, we try to test our own critical acuteness we ought to notice how we ourselves respond to wretched arguments which appear to justify the no doubt often very different conclusions which appeal most strongly to us.

1.44 A measure of symbolization is by now necessary. But before proceeding to that, something needs to be said about the word "racism," which has become as much a term of abuse as "democratic" is of praise. For unless the disputants in any debate as to whether some person or policy is or is not racist agree upon at least some rough and ready working definition of the key term, then in the most literal sense they simply do not know what they are talking about. Two points may usefully be made at this stage.

1.45 First, if you want to abominate racists as wicked, then the word "racism" will have to be defined as referring to a kind of bad behavior, presumably that of advantaging or disadvantaging individuals for no other and better reason than that they are members of one racially defined set rather than another. By the Axiom for Sets, formulated by Georg Cantor (1845–1918), the sole essential feature of a set is that its members have at least one common characteristic, which may be of any kind. The reason for introducing the word "set" here is that it does not carry the unwanted implications of such alternatives as "group" or "class" or "community."

1.46 The alternative hypothetical is that if, whether explicitly or implicitly, one defines the word "racism" as involving no more than the holding and/or expressing of beliefs in the existence of differences *on average* across one racially defined set as opposed to another, then the definition makes racism not a kind of bad behavior but a sort of disfavored belief. The crucial distinction here is between beliefs that *all* members of some racially defined set possess some characteristic and beliefs that some characteristic is *on average* more or less commonly possessed across one racially defined set than across another.

1.47 This is important. For from propositions expressing beliefs of the latter sort nothing can be validly inferred about the possession or nonpossession of the characteristic in question by any particular individual member of the racially defined set in question. You cannot, for instance, validly infer the height of any particular individual member of some human set from a proposition stating only the average height across that set. So even if some or many propositions of this kind are found to be true, their truth could not constitute a reasonable objection to our trying to discover every individual's merits or demerits directly, and then proceeding to treat him or her accordingly. The policies for which such discoveries really might carry upsetting implications are policies to secure the representation of various racially defined subsets of a population in various areas of activity and achievement in proportion to their numbers in that entire population. (For a leading lawyer's critique of attempts to enforce such policies by law, see Epstein 1992.)

1.48 Returning now to the business of symbolizing, what the fallacious arguments of 1.40 and 1.41 have in common is the following form: Given that *All so-and-so's are such-and-such* and given that *That is a such-and-such*, then it follows necessarily that *That is a so-and-so*. It is a very short and a space-saving further step to replace "so-and-so," "such-and-such," and "That" by letters. If you are going to do this, now and or later, then it is also a good idea to introduce the further notational refinement of distinguishing the subjects (the "so-and-so's") from the characteristics attributed to these subjects (that of being "such-and-such") by employing capital letters from the Latin alphabet for the former and lower-case Greek letters to symbolize the latter. Thus: If *All As are ø* (pronounced phī) and if *That is ø*, then it follows necessarily that *That is an A*; which, of course, it does not.

1.49 So much for the key notion of the form of an argument. Here and elsewhere all the particular specimens of any general class may be described as the several tokens of that same single type. ("Token" and "type" are a useful pair of labels that are well worth remembering.) The particular type or form of argument of which we have just been considering some tokens is fallacious. It has an unfortunately unmemorable traditional name: The Fallacy of the Undistributed Middle.

1.50 In the heyday of Senator Joseph McCarthy and of the House Committee on Un-American Activities, some favored the nickname "The Un-American Fallacy." This was a backhanded tribute to McCarthy and those members of his committee who were inclined to deduce that a person must be a Communist from the evidence that he possessed some characteristic perhaps shared by all Communists, but certainly not peculiar to them. This particular nickname is long since obsolete. Yet we still need to consider the point suggested by the pessimistic German philosopher Arthur Schopenhauer (1788–1860), although discounting his false and nasty insinuation that every defect from logical perfection is studied and designing: "It would be a good thing if every trick could receive some short and obviously appropriate name, so that when a man used this or that particular trick, he could be at once reproached for it" (Schopenhauer 1896, p. 18).

1.51 In the present context, the word "fallacy" does not refer to just any intellectual error. It is confined to one particular sort of such errors, that of mistaking an invalid argument for a valid one. This needs to be emphasized, since there is a common usage in which any misconception may be described as a fallacy. Thus, in the years immediately subsequent to the conclusion of World War II, many people in many countries were inclined to believe that any unwelcome large-scale events must be the effects of the explosion of atomic bombs. Those who held this belief to be mistaken could and did say, in accordance with this common usage, that it was a fallacy.

1.52 If it were only a matter of what is acceptable to dictionary makers as established and, hence, correct English usage, then the unbelievers could have rested their case for employing the word "fallacy," rather than the almost equally wounding "misconception," upon the undoubted propriety in these dictionary terms of the label "the Pathetic Fallacy." This label refers to the mistake of attributing to things which are not alive the feelings, dispositions, and reactions which can characterize only living things, in particular, people. But, in our stricter sense of the word "fallacy," neither this nor the putative misconception about the cause of those unwelcome large-scale events is a fallacy. The fallacy involved, if fallacy there was, must have been not the conclusion, but in the supporting argument. Having once mentioned The Pathetic Fallacy, if only incidentally, it is as well to seize the occasion to point out that the temptation to make mistakes of this kind lies in the fact that "Perhaps the simplest and most psychologically satisfying explanation of any observed phenomenon is that it happened that way because someone wanted it to happen that way" (Sowell 1986a, p. 97). But so very often in fact it did not.

1.53 In the case of the atomic bomb explosion hypothesis there very obviously was a fallacy involved, namely the fallacy of arguing that, simply because one series of events occurred after another series of events, the second series must have been caused by the first. This fallacy has been known traditionally—retaining the Latin, which was employed for all teaching and learning in the universities of medieval Europe—as the fallacy of arguing *post hoc ergo propter hoc* (after this therefore because of this). Until and unless someone is able to suggest a better English alternative, let us call it the Whatever-follows-must-be-the-consequence Fallacy.

1.54 The prime reasons for insisting upon the stricter usage of the term "fallacy" are efficiency and economy. We have in our rich language other words which can be used for just any kind of mistake or misconception. For a start there are the words "mistake" and "misconception." If we oafishly misemploy our verbal chisels as verbal screwdrivers, we thereby unfit them for the job to which they are best suited. So what do we use for a chisel when a chisel is what we need?

1.55 Compare another topical example far removed from our immediate interests. Those who have enjoyed such classic gangster movies as

The Roaring Twenties (1939) will remember that the word "hijack" was first introduced to refer to the forceful seizure of what was already stolen or in some other way contraband. There is surely nothing to be said for the current abusage, which makes "hijacking" an unappealing substitute for the good old word "piracy"—so romantically redolent of the Caribbean in an earlier century. It thus leaves us without any handy single word to distinguish the true present-day analogue of the original Prohibition phenomenon. Is not the case of forcible seizure by one criminal firm of a consignment of illicit drugs belonging to another, equally criminal competitor such an example?

1.56 It is for similar reasons that I have been following and shall continue to follow stricter usages of many other everyday terms. Such stricter usages are required even in making and maintaining the fundamental distinction between questions about truth or falsity and questions about validity or invalidity. Nor is there any call to go slumming in order to unearth examples of what we need to avoid. In his *Discourse on the Method,* René Descartes (1591–1650), who is by common consent recognized to have been the Father of Modern Philosophy, formulates his proposed doubt-proof, rock-bottom certainty as an argument: "I think, therefore I am." Yet he still affirms that this argument is something that he "clearly and distinctly conceives to be true" (Part IV). Allowance must of course be made in Descartes's case for the fact that he was writing in the early 1600s. But that is a reason why we have to do better. (By the way, the usual practice is to omit the definite article before the word "Method" in translating the title of this work from the original French. But that is wrong since Descartes clearly saw himself as developing and proclaiming the one and only correct method—his.)

1.57 Some other illustrations of the need for care in the employment of key terms have been given already. Care is also always required about knowledge and refutation. To say that someone knows something is to say more than that he claims to know it or that he believes it most strongly. It is to say also both that it is true and that he is in a position to know that it is true. So neither the sincerity of his conviction nor the ingenuousness of his utterance guarantees that he really knew. That is why the sarcastic tone enters our voices or why we write the key word between disclaiming quotation marks—in "sneer quotes"—when a man who has claimed to know turns out to have been wrong: "He 'knew' which horse was going to win the Kentucky Derby, but he 'knew' wrong." Nor in pointing out the falsity of the proposition that he asserted to be true is one necessarily challenging his integrity. It is most probably not that he was lying, just that he was honestly—and perhaps very expensively—mistaken.

1.58 To say that spokespersons for individuals or organizations refuted charges laid against those individuals or those organizations is to say much more than that they denied these charges and apparently believed that what they were saying was the truth. Rather, it is to say that they deployed sufficient evidencing reasons for believing that the charges were in fact false. If you do not want to say as much as that, then you should take the trouble to be noncommittal. You ought in that case to say only that these spokespersons claimed to have refuted the charges in question.

1.59 The same desire to husband resources of vocabulary, to preserve vital distinctions, should make us stingy in our application of the term "prejudice." Often it is treated as roughly equivalent to "opinion" or "conviction," albeit with powerful pejorative overtones. In this all-too-common abusage I have my opinions and my convictions, but you and he merely have prejudices—so called by me for no better reason than that they are yours or his and not mine. The word "prejudice" becomes a valuable extra item in the vocabulary of anyone striving to be more rational only when, and insofar as, it is employed scrupulously to pick out just those beliefs—whether right or wrong—that are either formed prior to proper consideration of the available evidence or else maintained in defiance of it.

1.60 It is obscurantist and demoralizing to apply the word "prejudice" in order to abuse other people's opinions, or even all strong convictions, simply as such. The judge who instructs the jury to consider carefully and without prejudice all and only the materials actually presented in court is not asking them to refuse to bring in a decisive verdict. Nor is there anything whatever wrong with anyone's opinions or with strong convictions, as such. What is obnoxious, and what merits all the abuse in the arsenal, is the willful maintaining of preconceptions against the weight of the evidence. But to do that is not an always incurable feature of the human condition. Nor is it the exclusive prerogative of other people.

1.61 Another occasionally useful distinction is that between the sense and the reference of some word or expression. The sense is the meaning and the reference is the object or objects to which the word or the expression refers; that is, the referent or the referents. The standard illustration for clarifying this distinction is provided by the expressions "the morning star" and "the evening star." The senses or meanings of these two expressions are obviously different. And when they were first introduced into the English language no one knew that they both have the same referent, namely the planet Venus. To emphasize this distinction between sense and reference, the useful convention is: when we are talking about the sense or meaning of some word or expression, to escort that word or that expression with quotation marks. But as long as words and expressions are being given their workaday employment of referring to referents, they remain unescorted. Another relevant convention is similarly to escort words and expressions with quotation marks when what is being talked about is neither their senses nor their referents, but the sounds made by their pronunciation, or indeed anything else but their meanings or their referents. For instance, we may in this way truly and clearly describe the words "cuckoo" and "sizzle" as onomatopoeic. We shall observe these conventions throughout this book and recommend readers always to do the same.

1.62 It is in terms of the distinction between sense and reference that we can explain the nature of what has traditionally been labeled the Masked Man Fallacy. It consists in arguing that because someone knows (or does not know) something under one description; therefore, they must know it (or therefore they cannot know it) as the same thing when it is considered under another description. So we cannot validly infer from the fact that someone was acquainted with what was called "the morning star" that they knew that it is identical with what was called "the evening star." Nor could we validly infer from the fact that someone was acquainted with a man who always wore a mask that the same person knew the identity of the man thus concerned to conceal his identity.

2

If/Then and All/None

2.1 Some examples in chapter 1 were, for good reasons given, trifling and even frivolous. Yet nothing could be more wrong than to carry away the impressions either that logic itself is trifling or that arguments cannot refer to matters of life and death. During World War II one of the soldiers of the doomed German Sixth Army outside Stalingrad wrote in what was to be his last letter to his wife: "If there is a God, you wrote to me in your last letter, then he will bring you back to me soon and healthy. . . . But, dearest, if your words are weighed now . . . you will have to make a difficult and great decision. . . ." (Schneider and Gullans 1965, p. 59).

2.2 The soldier was right. For if from any hypothesis, in this case that of the existence of (a certain sort of) God, you can validly deduce some consequence, in this case that a particular soldier will return "soon and healthy"; and if the consequence thus validly deduced is false, then it follows necessarily that the hypothesis itself must be false, too. So the wife, when she hears the news of the death of her husband, will indeed "have to make a difficult and great decision." She will have to decide whether simply to abandon the hypothesis or whether instead to reinterpret it so that it does not entail the kind of consequences which she had thought to be validly deduced therefrom.

2.3 In the one case she will argue: Since *If there were a God, then he would ensure that my husband would return safe from the wars* and since *My husband will not return safe from the wars*, then it follows necessarily that *There is no God*. In the other case she will, as we all must, accept that this last argument is valid. But she will now deny the truth of the conditional proposition, which functions as the first premise of that argument: *If there were (is) a God, then He would (will) ensure that my husband would (will) return safe from the wars*. What will be called continuing to believe in God will, therefore, involve for her both a fresh interpretation of the meaning of the word "God" and a correspondingly revised understanding of the nature of the Being to whom that word is by her intended to refer. Previously she must have been construing it in such a way that it followed, from a statement that *There is a God* and given the implicit acceptance of certain here unstated assumptions about the nature of that Being, that *He will ensure my husband's safe return*. But now she has come to interpret the same word "God" in such a way that this inference is invalid: there is, that is to say, no contradiction involved in, at one and the same time, both asserting these premises (properly understood) and denying the in fact false conclusion.

2.4 Arguments of the same form as that of the soldier at Stalingrad are employed wherever any hypothesis is tested, both in science proper and everywhere else. Sherlock Holmes, for instance, might argue: Since *If the thief entered this way, then there would be footprints in the flowerbed* and since *There are no footprints*, therefore, I deduce that *The thief did not enter this way*. The form of the argument, and it is a valid form, is: If *This is so*, then *That is so*; but *That is not so*; therefore, *This is not so* either. Since *This is so* and *That is so* are propositions and not subjects or predicates, it is sensible, if you want to introduce symbolism, to make your symbolism appropriately different from that suggested earlier for subjects and predicates (paragraph 1.48). The established convention is to use the lower case Latin letters p, q, and r. Since *This is not so* and *That is not so* are simply the denials or negations of, respectively, *This is so* and *That is so*, the further convention is to symbolize the negations of p, q, and r as, respectively, $\sim p$, $\sim q$, and $\sim r$ (read as *not p, not q,* and *not r*). Putting this new symbolism to work at once, we can now express the present valid form of argument as follows: *If p then q, but ~q, therefore ~p.*

2.5 Let us now distinguish this important and valid form from two other forms that are invalid. Let the two conditionals again be granted: *If there is a God, then the soldier will return*; and *If the thief entered this way, then there will be footprints in the flowerbed.* Now suppose: *The soldier has returned*; and *There are footprints in the flowerbed.* It will not do to infer from these pairs of premises the conclusions: *There is a God* and *The thief entered this way.* In such very simple cases, in which none of our public or private concerns are engaged, it is easy to see why it will not do. The crux is that the premises so far provided do not preclude the possibility of some alternative explanation. Even in a Godless world some soldiers would presumably return. So why not this one? And certainly had the thief entered this way, then the thief would have left footprints in the flowerbed. But nothing has so far been said to rule out the possibility that any footprints found there might have been made by someone other than the thief.

2.6 The second of the two invalid forms approaches from the opposite direction. Let the two conditionals be granted yet again: *If there is a God, then the soldier will return*; and *If the thief entered this way, then there will be footprints in the flowerbed.* But now suppose: *There is no God* and *The thief did not enter this way.* It will not do to infer from these fresh pairs of premises the conclusions: *The soldier will not return* and *There will be no footprints in the flowerbed.* The crux this time is that such conditionals say nothing about the situation on the alternative assumption that their antecedents are not true. It may well be true that *If one becomes a schoolteacher, then one will not succeed in amassing a fortune.* But, depressingly, this gives a person no positive reason to believe that he or she will be more successful in amassing a fortune even if choosing not to become a teacher.

2.7 Four possible moves can be made with such conditional propositions: two valid and two invalid. Some readers may find it helpful to run through the quadruplet systematically. But if for you the emphasis in this sort of foursome reel is too much on the word "reel," then skip to the next paragraph.

2.8 The valid move of arguing *If p then q, but ~q, therefore ~p* involves denying the consequent (the "then" bit) of the conditional to disprove the antecedent (the "if" bit): hence, Denying the Consequent.

The first invalid move, illustrated in paragraph 2.5, consists in arguing *If p then q, but q, therefore p.* This involves affirming the consequent in the baseless hope of thereby proving the antecedent: hence, Affirming the Consequent. A second valid move is too obvious and too obviously sound to require illustration. This is to argue: *If p then q, and p, therefore q.* In this we affirm the antecedent in order to prove the consequent: hence, for short, Affirming the Antecedent. The second invalid move completes the ring of changes. This invalid move, illustrated in paragraph 2.6, is to argue: *If p then q, but ~p, therefore ~q.* Here we deny the antecedent in the baseless hope of thereby disproving the consequent: hence, for short, Denying the Antecedent.

2.9 Important and fundamental questions about scientific method turn on elementary logical points expounded in the previous eight paragraphs. The heart of the matter lies in an asymmetry with regard to verification and falsification. Hypotheses are tested by deducing consequences which would follow if the hypothesis were true. When a hypothesis is tested and even one of its consequences is found in fact not to obtain, then that hypothesis, at least as originally formulated, is decisively demonstrated to have been false. Thus, the original hypothesis entertained by the soldier's wife (the hypothesis tested in the inferno of Stalingrad) was decisively disproved by her husband's death there. Holmes's hypothesis that the thief entered the house by a certain way was similarly falsified—shown, that is, to be false—when no footprints were found in the flowerbed. But when a hypothesis is tested and one of its consequences is in fact found to obtain, it is still not thereby demonstrated that the hypothesis must be true. Suppose that that German soldier had returned safe and sound. This would not have proved the existence of his wife's God. Nor would the discovery of footprints in the flowerbed have ruled out the possibility that these were made by someone else and that the thief used a different route to enter the house.

2.10 This asymmetry with respect to verification and falsification also characterizes such open universal propositions as *All swans are white* or *All living creatures are mortal.* These propositions are called "universal" because they refer to all the members of a class and "open" because the members of that class cannot be exhaustively listed. A single genuine counterexample is sufficient to disprove any such open universal proposition. But no matter how many confirming examples you produce, it is impossible to prove the open, universal proposition with any correspondingly decisive finality. It was this logical observation which led Francis Bacon (1561–1626) to make his often-quoted remark that "the force of the negative instance is greater." It was the same logical observation which provoked T. H. Huxley (1826–1895), a friend and defender of Charles Darwin (1809–1882), to speak of "The great tragedy of science—the slaying of a beautiful hypothesis by an ugly fact."

2.11 It was the observation of these logical asymmetries that served as one foundation of Sir Karl Popper's enormously influential and salutary philosophy of science. No open universal proposition can ever be confirmed beyond all conceivable future correction, although some can be decisively and finally disproved. Yet the crucial elements in every imaginable scientific theory, and any acceptable candidates for the status of law of nature, must be propositions of this kind. So Popper drew the exciting moral that science is and can only be a matter of endless striving and of endless inquiry. The best we have or ever could have can and could only be the best so far (Magee 1973 and Popper 1959 and 1963).

2.12 This is all very well if it is taken to mean only that there will always be more for scientists to discover. But Popper himself, by failing to make and employ the crucial distinction between two senses of the word "possible," became trapped in the intolerably contradictory position both of maintaining that there is no such thing as real, certain knowledge and of glorying in the enormous and wide-ranging advances in scientific knowledge. Thus, in *The Logic of Scientific Discovery* (1959) he asserted that "The old scientific idea of *episteme* [the Greek word for knowledge]—of absolutely certain, demonstrable knowledge—has proved to be an idol. . . . Every scientific statement must remain tentative for ever. . . ." (pp. 280–81). He nevertheless later published a book entitled *Objective Knowledge: An Evolutionary Approach* (Popper 1972).

2.13 Possibilities may be either logical or practical. To say that some occurrence is logically possible, that it is conceivable, is to say only that it is possible to provide a coherent and intelligible description of what would be happening if that logically possible occurrence were actually to occur. That somebody should jump over the Statue of Liberty

is conceivable, that is, logically possible. But everyone knows that it is
practically impossible. Therefore, to show that no open universal proposition can ever be confirmed beyond all logical possibility of future correction—which is what in effect Popper did show—is not to show that
such scientific propositions cannot, in the ordinary understanding of the
word "know," be known to be true. For in that understanding, to be
known a proposition does not have to be demonstrated. That is, it does
not have to be shown that to deny that proposition would be to contradict yourself. It is sufficient that it should in fact be true and that the
person claiming to know it either possesses sufficient evidencing reason
or is otherwise in a position justifiably to claim to know it.

2.14 As the ancient Greeks used to say of their greatest poet: "Even
Homer sometimes nods." So we should be distressed but not surprised
to discover that Popper once supplied us with an interesting example of
the fallacy of Denying the Antecedent. Yet the right lesson to learn from
this embarrassing lapse is utterly Popperian. It is the need for unresting
critical alertness—perhaps especially in our attention to those with
whom we most agree and whom we most admire.

2.15 The lapse occurs when Popper is reconsidering that medieval
favorite, *All men are mortal*. He remarks that this "mortal" ought to be
construed as "liable to die." This is certainly true. It was because they
were in fact construing it as (naturally) "liable to die," that those who
believed in the (miraculous) translation both of the prophet Elijah and
of Mary the mother of Jesus rightly refused to accept these as counterexamples. The claim that these two exceptional people were by a
miraculous overriding of the laws of nature taken straight up into heaven
does not deny, but takes it for granted, that they, too, like all other
humans, were naturally liable to death. But for those miracles they, too,
would in due course have died ordinary, unprivileged, natural deaths.
Popper next proceeds to report that it was "part of Aristotle's theory that
every generated creature is bound to decay and die. . . . But this theory
was refuted by the discovery that bacteria are not bound to die, since
multiplication by fission is not death . . ." (Popper 1972, p. 10). Certainly from the hypothesis that *All living things are bound to decay and
die* we can deduce: first, *All bacteria are bound to decay and die*; second,
All humans are bound to decay and die; and so on indefinitely. And cer-

tainly the falsity of the first of these consequents is sufficient to show the falsity of that antecedent. But this is fallacious to argue from the falsity of that antecedent to the falsity of any of those consequents.

2.16 The facts, first, that *All men are mortal* is indeed a consequence of *All living things (including men) are mortal,* and, second, that because of the splitting bacteria the latter proposition is now known to be false, are not sufficient reasons for saying that the former proposition must be false also. Suppose they were sufficient. Then to refute any theory would be simultaneously to refute all the propositions deducible from that theory, and hence all the propositions it was capable of explaining. This would carry a curious and a catastrophic consequence. Any established theory which is refuted is refuted through its failure to explain recalcitrant facts. And it would surely be unusual and certainly scandalous if a theory were to have become established notwithstanding that it could not explain any even of the facts already known in its heyday. On the present supposition, however, by refuting any established theory we should be left with nothing for any new theory to explain except the fresh facts deployed in that very refutation—which is absurd.

2.17 The four moves listed systematically in paragraph 2.8 can be further illuminated with the aid of distinctions between necessary and sufficient conditions, distinctions far and away more valuable than any of the eminently forgettable technicalities of that paragraph. The purpose of the next four paragraphs, therefore, is to explain the logical structure of those four moves and the logical relations between them by first explaining and then employing the notions of logically necessary and logically sufficient conditions. Those in no mind to mind their p's and q's should skip at once to paragraph 2.22.

2.18 When given the truth of one proposition p the truth of another proposition q follows necessarily, then the truth of p is, by definition, a logically sufficient condition of the truth of q. That Bertie is an Englishman is thus a logically sufficient condition of the truth that Bertie is a man. When some proposition r necessarily cannot be true unless some other proposition s is also true, then the truth of s is, again by definition, a logically necessary condition of the truth of r. That Cynthia has been married is a logically necessary condition of the truth of the proposition that Cynthia is divorced. You could not even begin to get divorced unless you have first been married.

2.19 It should be obvious that to say that p is a logically sufficient condition of q is not to say either that p is the only logically sufficient condition of q or that it is a logically necessary condition of q. Since Frenchmen are also men, that Bertie is a Frenchman would be an alternative, logically sufficient condition of the truth that Bertie is a man. For the same good and sufficient reason it is not a logically necessary condition of the truth that Bertie is a man that Bertie is an Englishman.

2.20 Again, to say that s is a logically necessary condition of r is not to say either that s is the only logically necessary condition of r or that it is a logically sufficient condition of r. Since it is not the case—even for countries with high divorce rates, such as Sweden and the United States—that everyone who gets married gets divorced, either forthwith or eventually, it may well be true that Cynthia has married and has not been divorced. And even if everyone getting married proceeded at once to divorce, to say that someone has married would be to say less than to say he or she is now divorced. Thus, that Cynthia was married is a logically necessary but not the only logically necessary nor the logically sufficient condition of her now being divorced. (Many of us, however, must have known marriages of which it would have been fair, though unseemly, to comment: "Well, I suppose marriage is a logically necessary precondition of divorce.")

2.21 Putting the distinction between necessary and sufficient conditions immediately to work, we can say that the two fallacies represent misunderstandings of what it is for one proposition to be any sort of sufficient condition of another. For to say *If p then q* is to say simply that p is some sort of sufficient condition of q. The second invalid move, to argue *If p then q, but ~p, therefore ~q* confounds this initial statement that p is a sufficient condition of q with the claim that p is a necessary condition of q. Were p indeed a necessary condition of q then we could infer $\sim q$ from $\sim p$. The first invalid move, to argue *If p then q, but q, therefore p*, confounds the same initial statement that p is a sufficient condition of q with the claim that p is the only sufficient and necessary condition of q. Were p indeed the only sufficient and necessary condition of q then we could infer p from q. Or, in other words, this second fallacy consists in the confusion of *If p then q* with *If and only if p then q*. Since English—like, so far as I know, all other natural languages—lacks a single word for "if and only if," logicians have invented the artificial and seemingly misspelled vocable "iff." In these terms this second fallacy of Denying the Antecedent can be characterized as the mistake of deducing from *If p then q* what would indeed follow from *Iff p then q*.

2.22 If things seem to have been moving either too fast or too abstractedly in the five previous paragraphs, and especially if you think of yourself as a student rather than as a general reader, then you would be well advised to settle down with a pencil and paper to run through, in your own way and at your own pace, the various logical points about conditionals treated in all the first sixteen paragraphs of this chapter. Half the point of having and using the simple symbolism introduced in paragraph 2.4 and the symbols introduced earlier in paragraph 1.48 is to make this sort of checking easier and quicker. (The other half is to escape the often misleading distractions of individual interests in, and beliefs about, some of the particular propositions which may have served as premises or conclusions in some argument offered as an example for examination.) Certainly no one can reasonably expect to acquire any facility even with this very modest minimum of symbolism without undertaking a little private practice of this sort. In general, any argument which is either difficult or contentious should be examined closely and in writing. It is altogether too easy—even when the intentions of all concerned are impeccable, which is not always the case—for the swiftness and fleetingness of the spoken word to deceive the mind. And just because what is not recorded is not recorded, everyone's ground may shift without anyone noticing it.

2.23 Suppose someone says, as someone often does: *If I (Jones) do not obtain some much-desired good then there is no justice in this world.* And suppose, as sometimes happens, *Jones does obtain that much-desired good.* Are we entitled from these two premises alone to infer the conclusion which someone else is sure now to point out to Jones: that *There is some justice in the world*? Certainly this conclusion is true, and perhaps justice did indeed demand that Jones should obtain that much-desired good. But this argument as an argument—and that is what we are talking about—is invalid. It is an instance of (attempting to disprove the consequent by) Denying the Antecedent.

2.24 There are three reasons why it is perhaps not immediately obvious that the particular argument about Jones is fallacious. First, the proposed conclusion is true; second, we get hazed by the negatives in both antecedent and consequent; and, third, the fact that justice was done on this occasion—assuming it was—is by itself and without recourse to any other argument a sufficient reason for saying that *There is some justice in the world*. We remove all three difficulties if we get that pencil and paper, and write down: *p = I (Jones) do not obtain this*; and *q = There is no justice in this world*. Given these interpretations of *p* and *q* we can now symbolize the argument: *If p then q, but ~p, therefore ~q*. And this is manifestly a form of argument the invalidity of which we came fully to appreciate earlier; especially in paragraphs 2.6, 2.8, 2.14–2.16, and 2.18–2.19. Of course, we also have to appreciate that with these interpretations of *p* and *q*, the negations *~p* and *~q* become, respectively, *Jones obtains this* and *There is some justice in the world*. The rule is that double negation, "not not," cancels out, leaving no negation at all.

2.25 There is another sort of distinction between necessary and sufficient conditions that is of great practical importance. When we say that *p* is a logically sufficient condition of *q*, then we are saying that we could not assert *p* and deny *q* without contradicting ourselves. But when *such-and-such* is said to be not the logically but the causally sufficient condition of *this or that*, then what is being said is: In the world as it actually is, with the laws of nature what they actually are, *such-and-such* could not be produced or occur without producing *this or that*. When *such-and-such* is said to be not the logically but the causally necessary condition of *this or that*, then what is being said is: In the world as it actually is, with the laws of nature as they actually are, *this or that* could not occur or be produced without *such-and-such* first occurring or being produced.

2.26 Suppose that heavy smoking is, for people in certain circumstances, people having certain constitutions, and people who do not happen to die of something else first, a causally sufficient condition of eventually contracting lung cancer. Then this means that heavy smoking guarantees eventual lung cancer for those people, in those circumstances, and always assuming that they do not die of something else first. But it does not mean that heavy smoking is either a causally necessary or a causally sufficient condition guaranteeing that every heavy smoker will eventually contract lung cancer if he or she does not die of something else first. For there certainly are—although this appears very unjust to many of my fellow never-smokers—some lung cancer victims who have never smoked at all. Equally certainly our Greek contemporaries, who are the heaviest smokers in Europe, nevertheless have one of the lowest lung cancer rates in the world. (It is perhaps just worth noting as a sign of our times that investigation of the possible causes of this Greek immunity appears to have been inhibited as politically incorrect. It is no doubt thought in some quarters that those who rebelliously persist in defying official campaigns against smoking deserve to die of it.)

2.27 It is, however, not contradictory to suggest that what happen to be in our world either causally sufficient or causally necessary conditions would in a different universe be neither. Or, putting exactly the same point in different words, there is nothing inconceivable about the idea of a universe governed by quite different laws from those which seemingly govern our actual universe. Or, in yet other words again, the occurrence of an event which must be, according to these actual laws, physically impossible is by no means by that token logically impossible (see paragraphs 1.25 and 1.26). Indeed there seems to be no contradiction in the suggestion of a universe not governed by any laws at all—a point made, to the great scandal of the philosophical public, by David Hume (1711–1776) in *A Treatise of Human Nature* (I [iii] 3).

2.28 In order to put this distinction between causally necessary and causally sufficient conditions to work at once, let us consider an argument offered by a pair of contributors to a widely circulated volume of papers on educational theory. They were attacking the proposition that heredity matters. The argument concerns all kinds of achievement and not, therefore, only one kind of ability or disposition. "The model, and especially [Francis] Galton's version of it, of course denies the possibility of change . . . if 80 percent of adult performance is directly dependent upon genetic inheritance, how have the styles of our lives and patterns of our thinking changed to the extent that they have?" (Richardson and Spears 1972, p. 74).

2.29 This objection, which its proud authors obviously regarded as knockdown decisive, is simply irrelevant. For what their opponents were maintaining was that some appropriate level of ability is a causally necessary condition of every kind of achievement and that what abilities are available to each individual is largely determined—to the extent of about 80 percent—by that individual's heredity. They were most certainly not maintaining that having the necessary inherited measure of ability is a causally sufficient condition of reaching the appropriate level of achievement. To put it coarsely, what those opponents held was not (1) that silk purses are born not made, but (2) that you cannot make silk purses out of sows' ears. The objection offered here would be decisive against that first thesis. But against the second it has no weight at all.

2.30 The citing of this supposed refutation here is not, however, a contribution to the ongoing debate about how far the differences in performance between individuals and between sets of individuals is to be explained by reference to their genes and how far by reference to their environments. Rather, it is to use this supposed refutation as an example of a dispute in which one party maintains an extreme position and the other does not, and to indicate the temptations to which the parties in such disputes are exposed.

2.31 If we ourselves are committed to an extreme position then we are apt to assume or to pretend—to borrow the phrase General Robert E. Lee employed to refer to his opponents in the Union armies during the American Civil War—that "those people," our opponents, also are. Thus those inclined to hold that everything is environmentally determined become, for that very reason, tempted either to assume or to pretend that anyone who disagrees with them must hold that nothing is environmentally determined. Certainly, if this polarization assumption were universally true, it would make it easier for all spokesmen of extreme positions to dispose of the thus correspondingly extreme positions of their opponents, hence the strength of the temptation. But the controversial world is not so conveniently arranged, with this sort of ideal balance. In the present case, for instance, there never have been—and for very good reason—any extreme hereditarians maintaining that our genetic constitutions are the sufficient conditions of all that we are and can be. But there certainly are at this time many environmentalist ultras. These people do want to hold that everything about us—or as near as makes precious little matter everything—is determined by our environments. (For some citations from spokespersons for such extreme environmentalism see, for instance, the introduction to Flew 1997.)

2.32 These points about the temptations of extremism neither depend upon nor warrant any general contention that we ought to strive for moderation in the content of all our opinions, or that truth is always in the middle. Suppose that it had been, say, President John F. Kennedy and not, as it was, Senator Barry Goldwater, who said: ". . . extremism in the defense of liberty is no vice . . . moderation in the pursuit of justice is no virtue" (Acceptance speech at the Republican National Convention, July 16, 1964). Then all of America's liberals—and not they alone—would have endorsed these splendid words. Such hypothetical endorsers would have been right. We should be right to concur anyway. Again, it actually was Abraham Lincoln himself who warned: "Let us not be diverted by more of these sophistical contrivances wherewith we are so industriously plied and belabored—contrivances such as groping for some middle ground between the right and the wrong" (Speech at the Cooper Union, New York City, February 27, 1860).

2.33 The alleged truism that truth is always in the middle is not merely false but demonstrably false. If, as this silly and unprincipled principle requires, the truth really were, for all values of A and Z, midway between A and Z; then it must also be, according to the requirements of the same principle, halfway between the halfway point between A and Z and Z; and so on, indefinitely. This conclusion is incoherent and absurd. The same must therefore apply to the principle from which it is thus validly deduced: The Truth-is-always-in-the-middle Damper.

2.34 This abstract theoretical demonstration has concrete practical relevance. For there are in fact a great many people who adopt as one of their main guiding principles the principle that they should, with regard to all controverted issues of belief, strive to position themselves equidistant between whatever they see as the most extreme opposing standpoints currently adopted. Not only does this principle, for reasons just now stated or suggested, guarantee commitments to error of all kinds. It also—paradoxically—exposes its protagonists to manipulation from those very extremes which it professes to eschew. Persuasive operators, discerning this common affection for whatever can be presented as the middle ground, can and do find ways of shifting the apparent center in whatever direction they desire.

2.35 Such persuasive operators strive to make out that the position which they want the subjects of their persuadings to adopt is located roughly halfway between two opposite extremes. This sort of manipulation of people who want always to be soberly and levelheadedly in the middle is in the sphere of belief and persuasion closely analogous to a universally familiar and too often successful bargaining strategy. This is the strategy whereby one side makes inordinate demands in order that any splittings of the difference fifty-fifty shall yield a result going further its way than the way of the other.

2.36 Whatever may be the case in bargaining situations, where the object just is to get more or less of whatever it may be, it is quite different where the aim is—or ought to be—to discover truth. When discovering truth is the object, then considerations of moderation or extremism are as such neither here nor there. They can in consequence find purchase in some particular context only insofar as we happen to have some substantial independent reason to believe that in that context either a moderate thesis or an extreme one is more likely to be true.

2.37 There are, as we have just been noticing (see paragraphs 2.32–2.35), insidious dangers and temptations in what presents itself or is presented as the middle ground. The temptation of the extremist, on the other hand, is to assume or to pretend that everyone else is committed to some equally extreme opposite position (see paragraph 2.31). The particular extremists who occasioned this comment believed (see paragraphs 2.28–2.29), or at least wanted to believe, that *All human differences are determined by the environment.* To disagree with this it is sufficient to assert no more than that *Not all human differences are determined by the environment.* The first of these two propositions is a universal proposition and the second is its contradictory. But, as we have seen (e.g., paragraph 2.10), any universal proposition can be decisively falsified and its contradictory equally decisively verified by the production of even one single genuine counterexample. (A proposition which is the contrary proposition or the contradictory proposition of another proposition is always known simply as its contrary or its contradictory.) Yet our extremists, perhaps on the basis of an invalid argument, and for certain mistakenly, assumed that their opponents are committed to the correspondingly extreme and diametrically opposite thesis that *No human differences are determined by the environment.*

2.38 This third proposition, which Logicians somewhat misleadingly dub the contrary of the first, is like that first, itself, but unlike the second, universal. It, too, therefore, is exposed to definitive falsification by the production of a single genuine counterexample. So the protagonists of the first proposition, *All human differences are determined by the environment*, are bound to see their controversial task as easier if they believe or pretend to believe that they have to refute only the third proposition, *No human differences are determined by the environment,* rather than the second proposition, *Not all human differences are determined by the environment.* Nevertheless, as must by now be obvious, it is fallacious to argue that because someone denies the first proposition and hence is committed to the second, therefore, they must in consistency assert the third. For the contradictory is not the contrary.

2.39 The distinction between contraries and contradictories is crucially important in debates in which at least one party is maintaining that something is for that party a matter of principle. The first thing to get clear, and this is not always easily done, is precisely what the supposed principle actually is. If it really is a principle, then the persons proclaiming it must be maintaining either that *all* or that *no* so-and-sos ought to be such-and-such. For some people, for example, it is a matter of principle that all schools, or at any rate all tax-funded schools, should be comprehensive (i.e., nonselective) neighborhood schools. By this principle, which these people may well wish to describe as the principle of comprehension, they necessarily become committed to opposing the establishment or, if already established, the continuation of any schools of any other kind.

2.40 The temptation for these people is to argue that any opponents who favor the establishment or, if already established, the continuation of any schools not of their own single approved kind thereby concede what they themselves see as the principle of comprehension. But opponents of that principle may be, and most likely are, simply contradicting it. In that case, all that they are denying is that *all* schools ought to be of that one, or perhaps any, particular kind. They are not necessarily, and probably are not, in fact, maintaining the contrary principle: that there should be *no* such schools.

2.41 As a more stimulatingly controversial example, consider the principle to which Davy Crockett was appealing when he told his colleagues in the Congress of the United States: "We have the right, as individuals, to give away as much of our own money as we please in charity; but as members of Congress we have no right to appropriate a dollar of the public money." That principle, of course, was that Congress possessed no rights or powers other than those granted to it by the Constitution. And Davy Crockett, like President James Madison, could not "undertake to lay my finger on that article of the Constitution which grants a right to Congress of expending, on objects of benevolence, the money of their constituents."

3

Evasion and Falsification

3.1 Imagine some aggressively nationalistic Scotsman settled down one Sunday morning with his customary copy of that shock-horror tabloid *The News of the World*. He reads the story under the headline, "Sidcup Sex Maniac Strikes Again." Our reader is, as he confidently expected, agreeably shocked: "No Scot would do such a thing!" Yet the very next Sunday he finds in that same favorite source a report of the even more scandalous ongoings of Mr. Angus MacSporran in Aberdeen. This clearly constitutes a perfect counterexample, one which definitively falsifies the universal proposition originally put forward. ("Falsifies" here is the opposite of "verifies"; and it therefore means "shows to be false.") Allowing that this is indeed such a counterexample, he ought to withdraw, retreating perhaps to a rather weaker claim about most or some Scotsmen. But even an imaginary Scot is, like the rest of us, human; and none of us always does what we ought to do. So instead he amends his statement to: "No true Scotsman would do such a thing!"

3.2 An equally simple but actual example of this No-true-Scotsman Move was provided by Stokely Carmichael during the early days of the Black Power movement. On a visit to London he was arguing the thesis that the world is now divided between exploiting white and exploited colored people. "What about [Fidel] Castro?" asked one member of his audience. "What about Che Guevara?" "I don't," retorted Mr. Carmichael, "consider them white." (He did not, at least on that occasion, follow his Black Power associate James Baldwin by explaining that, for him, "whiteness is a state of mind, not a complexion.")

3.3 In these two textbook examples it is immediately obvious what is going on, and what is wrong. A bold, indeed reckless, claim about all those who happen to be members of a certain category is being surreptitiously replaced by an utterance which is, in effect, made true by an arbitrary redefinition. If anyone who satisfies all the ordinary requirements for being accounted a Scot behaves like the Sidcup sex maniac, then our aggressively nationalistic Scot will take that fact as by itself sufficient reason to disqualify that person from rating as a true Scot. True Scots are, by his implicit definition, not sex maniacs. Likewise, if any people who would conventionally be accounted Caucasians commended themselves to Mr. Carmichael, then that fact alone became for Mr. Carmichael a decisive reason against considering those exceptional Caucasians to be truly white.

3.4 If all examples of the No-true-Scotsman Move were as simple and straightforward as these two, then there might perhaps have been little need to introduce such a label. But they are not. So more needs to be said. The essence of the move consists in sliding between two radically different interpretations of the same or very similar forms of words. In one, in this case the original interpretation, what is asserted is synthetic and contingent. In the other, in this case the later and highly factitious interpretation, what we have is a custom-built necessary truth. This fundamental distinction can be brought out and fixed securely in mind with the help of William Shakespeare. Questioned about what the ghost said, Hamlet replies:

> There's ne'er a villain dwelling in all Denmark
> But he's an arrant knave.

His friend Horatio responds:

> There needs no ghost, my lord, come from the grave
> To tell us this. (*Hamlet* 1.5)

3.5 There needs no ghost because Hamlet's proposition is analytic and logically necessary. What makes it analytic is that its truth can be known simply by analyzing the meanings of all its constituent terms. What makes it a logically necessary truth is that to deny it would involve self-contradiction: Its contradictory would be a logically necessary falsehood. It is an apriori truth, one which could be known to be true without reference to what does or does not in fact happen in this universe as it actually is. Instead of this, and very reasonably, Horatio wanted a synthetic and logically contingent proposition; one the truth or falsity of which could not be known merely by fully understanding its meaning, and the contradictory of which would be neither necessarily true nor necessarily false. He wanted not an apriori but an aposteriori truth. Had Hamlet claimed—however anachronistically and irrelevantly to Shakespeare's dramatic purposes—that all Danish villains were the products of maternal deprivation, then his proposition would have been not analytic but synthetic, not necessary but contingent. It would also have been aposteriori, inasmuch as it could be known to be true—if it were true—only by reference to some actual study of the deprived home background of Danish villains.

3.6 I write both "apriori" and "aposteriori" as single, unitalicized words deliberately. It is chauvinistically, you might even say bigotedly, purist to treat as unnaturalized aliens immigrants first landed over a quarter of a millennium ago. But it may perhaps help in remembering the meanings of these two contrasting terms to say that both "apriori" and "aposteriori" derive from Latin, the former meaning from before or earlier and the latter meaning from after or later.

3.7 If we put things in terms of this fundamental distinction between the apriori and the aposteriori, then the No-true-Scotsman Move consists in responding to the falsification of a contingent proposition by covertly so reinterpreting the words in which it was originally formulated that these now become the expression of an arbitrarily constructed necessary truth. This maneuver always involves either a high or a low redefinition of a crucial term. Where the qualifications for membership of the class are increased, we have a high redefinition. Where they are reduced, we have a low redefinition. To rate as a true Scot you have to be not merely a Scot but a Scot who is not a sex maniac. To score—if that is the word— as one of the hateful exploiters you have to be not merely a Caucasian but a Caucasian who is not a Latin American Communist. What must have been an example of the low redefinition of the word "socialist" was provided by the British Queen Victoria's eldest son, the future King Edward VII, when he—of all people—said in a speech at the Mansion House, in the City of London, the financial center of the then–British Empire: "We are all socialists nowadays" (November 5, 1895).

3.8 The temptation here is not just to slide, under the pressure of falsification, from an interpretation of some form of words which construes it as expressing a contingent to one which construes it as expressing a necessary proposition. It is to fail to recognize what has happened and, hence, to be apt to slide back again into the original interpretation immediately after that pressure is removed. Our Scottish nationalist is all too likely to go away believing that his original overconfidence in Scottish superiority has been vindicated; while Mr. Carmichael's starkly confrontational picture of the world was in his own mind probably preserved without the revision which he himself had in his own way admitted that the existence of the Castro regime made necessary. It is important to be aware of the possibility of analogous equivocations even where we have not been alerted by a flagrant No-true-Scotsman Move (see paragraphs 1.14–1.15).

3.9 Suppose, for instance, that someone assures us that all criminal behavior or all sexual deviation or all suicidal desires and decisions are symptomatic of mental disease. Such things are said frequently nowadays, and not least by people paid to know about mental disease and mental health. The first question to press upon such psychiatric spokespersons, before we begin to ask whether what is said is true, is What sort of thing actually is being said? Are we really confronted by a genuine contingent claim, or is it all ultimately a matter of definition and of more or less arbitrarily chosen criteria? That is to say, are these spokespersons claiming to have made a discovery; the discovery perhaps that all those who commit crimes are also, by quite independent criteria, mentally diseased? Or is it that they are taking the committing of a crime as itself a criterion of mental disease, and in effect insisting that such behavior constitutes a logically sufficient condition (see paragraphs 2.18–2.21) of being mentally diseased? In that case it would for them be contradictory to say that a man is committing a crime and yet is not mentally diseased.

3.10 In short, is it as it used to be when suicide under English law was still a crime? Then juries, without hearing any expert psychiatric evidence, regularly returned the verdict: suicide, while the balance of the mind was disturbed. The reason for returning these unevidenced verdicts was to protect the suicides' heirs from the loss of their inheritances. For it was illegal for anyone to benefit in consequence of either their own or of someone else's crime. (For substantial discussion of the concepts of mental disease and mental health see, for instance, Flew 1993, chapter 7.)

3.11 Consider another example, which again illustrates the importance of distinguishing between analytic necessary and synthetic contingent interpretations of the same form of words. It is provided by an argument which has been widely current since as early as 1651, the year in which Thomas Hobbes (1588–1679) published his *Leviathan*. Whether or not Hobbes himself did ever present this argument, it certainly was thereafter generally credited—or perhaps we should say discredited—to him. The premise is that all actions must as such be motivated. But in that case, it is urged, that all actions are performed and could only be performed because the agent wants to perform them. Since to do always exactly what you want to do regardless of the proper claims of anyone else is to be utterly selfish, it appears to follow that there is and could be no such thing as an unselfish action.

3.12 Wait a minute! The premise is presumably construed as analytic and necessary. Certainly no other grounds are offered why we should accept it as true. But the conclusion is equally certainly put forward as a scandalous and demoralizing revelation. This by itself is enough to show that there must be something wrong. It cannot be right to infer a substantial conclusion from a merely tautological premise. Exactly what is going wrong and how it is going wrong can best be seen by displaying the ambiguity of the crucial term "want." In the premise to want is simply to have a desire or a motive, any desire or motive at all. It is only this equation which permits us to go on to say that all actions "are performed and could only be performed because the agent wants to perform them." But in the conclusion "to do always and only exactly what you want to do" has to be taken in a different and stronger sense: the sense in which someone might claim to have gone to visit a sick relative although that person did not at all want to do so. It is only in this interpretation that the proposed conclusion becomes exciting and surprising and carries the shocking implication that "there is and could be no such thing as an unselfish action." So construed it is, however, not supported by the premise; and in any case, as my illustration must have suggested, it is known to be false.

3.13 Here it is desirable also to distinguish between self-interest and selfishness. To say that someone's conduct was selfish is to say more than that it was self-interested. For selfishness is always and necessarily to be condemned. But surely self-interest is not? For example, when two healthy siblings eagerly eat their dinners, it would presumably be correct to say that each is in this matter pursuing his or her self-interest. Yet this is no sufficient reason to start reproaching them. The time for that would be after brother has grabbed and eaten his sister's dinner as well as his own or has perhaps in some less flagrant way refused to respect the proper claims of someone else. Even when my success can be gained only at the cost of the failure of others, it would be inordinately austere to insist that it is always and necessarily selfish for me to pursue my own self-interest. For is anyone prepared to assert that all rival candidates competing for appointment to some coveted position are culpably selfish in not withdrawing in order to clear the way for the others?

3.14 The failure, or rather the willful refusal, to observe the distinction between self-interest and selfishness is the prime source of perennial misrepresentations of Adam Smith (1723–1790) and his followers as apostles of selfish greed. Certainly the Nobel laureate Chicago economist George Stigler was absolutely right to describe Smith's *Inquiry into the Nature and Causes of the Wealth of Nations* (1776) as "a stupendous edifice erected upon the granite of self-interest." But even if anyone has tried, certainly no one has succeeded in finding in that work any passage advocating selfishness. And there is, inevitably and obviously, much to the contrary in Smith's other masterpiece, *The Theory of the Moral Sentiments* (1759).

3.15 A third example of alternations between analytic necessary and synthetic contingent interpretations of the same or very similar forms of words is provided by Joan Rockwell's *Fact in Fiction* (1974), a work boldly subtitled *The Use of Literature in the Systematic Study of Society*. In the preface she writes: "My basic premise is that literature neither 'reflects' nor 'arises from' society, but rather is an integral part of it, and should be recognized as being as much so as any institution, the Family for instance, or the State" (p. vii). So long as this is interpreted as in effect a matter of definition, it is clearly only too true. But in her very next sentence she slips toward a more substantial interpretation of this "basic premise." In it she asserts: "Narrative fiction is an indicator, by its form and content, of the morphology [shape] and nature of a society. . . ." In the main body of the book we find that first denial completely forgotten. It is no longer false but, it seems, necessarily true that literature "reflects" the society within which it arises: "To say that writers necessarily reflect their own times, which I must repeat is the justification for using their fictions to study the facts of their society, is to say that they are bound to do so, and cannot choose to do otherwise" (ibid., p. 119).

3.16 It is one thing, and quite indisputable, to say that anything which happens in society is, by definition, a social phenomenon: "my basic premise is that literature . . . is an integral part of" the society in which it is produced. But it is quite another thing, and not one to be accepted without the deployment of a deal of evidence, to say that literary products always contain information about the societies in which they were produced: "writers necessarily reflect their own times." Maybe they do. Maybe it is impossible for even the best of historical novelists or of science fiction writers to cover their parochial social tracks. But to show this it is certainly not sufficient to appeal to the quasidefinitional truth that the production of literature is a social phenomenon.

3.17 The last thirteen paragraphs (3.4–3.16) have explained the fundamental distinction between logically contingent and logically necessary propositions and have shown how, by failing to observe it, we can be most powerfully tempted fallaciously to infer substantial, logically contingent conclusions from premises constitutionally incapable of yielding conclusions of that kind. The No-true-Scotsman Move is an attempt to evade falsification. Through it a piece of sleight of mind replaces a contingent by a logically necessary proposition. We need next to relate the criticism of such maneuvers with the Popperian ideas presented and criticized in chapter 2 (see especially paragraphs 2.10–2.13), and by these means bring out why any such maneuver is inconsistent with a forthright concern for truth.

3.18 The heart of the matter is that the substance and extent of any assertion always is and must be exactly proportionate to the substance and extent of the corresponding denial necessarily involved in the making of that assertion. To assert a proposition is as such to deny the contradictory of that proposition (p is therefore equivalent to the negation of the negation of p, symbolized as $p \equiv {\sim}{\sim}p$). So the more you want to say, the more you have to stick out your neck. The wider and the more substantial your claims, and the greater the scope and the explanatory power of the theory which you propose, the greater must be the range of theoretically possible occurrences which would, if they actually occurred, falsify your claims or your theory. In the words of a fine Spanish proverb: " 'Take what you like,' said God, 'take it, and pay for it.' "

3.19 The No-true-Scotsman Move can thus be seen as one of too many alternative maneuvers attempting to get hold of a big dollop of substantial truth without paying for it. The original contingent claim was wide and substantial. What it denied made it falsifiable by the misbehavior of any Scot; and we are supposing it actually was falsified by the deplorable conduct of our imaginary Mr. Angus MacSporran. The substitute assertion was not in the same way substantial. Precisely because it could not be falsified by any describable occurrences, it was not really making any assertion at all about what does or does not happen in the universe around us. This is what was meant when, in that enigmatic masterpiece, the *Tractatus Logico-Philosphicus* (1922), Ludwig Wittgenstein (1889–1951) wrote: "The propositions of logic are tautologies. The propositions of logic therefore say nothing. (They are the analytical propositions.)" (§§ 6.1–6.11).

3.20 The logical observation of paragraph 3.18 constitutes another element in the Popperian philosophy of science, which, as we saw in chapter 2 (see paragraph 2.11), insisted that "The best we have or ever could have can and could only be the best so far." That surely too absolute rejection of all ultimacy in science, a rejection inspired especially by Albert Einstein's overthrowing of the Newtonian establishment, constitutes no license to abandon the critical pursuit of truth. Quite the reverse is true. Certainly science requires openness and bold conjectures. But the openness required is openness to the possibility of new and possibly upsetting discoveries of what actually is the case, while the conjectures must be conjectures about what is in fact true. And, as I have been urging, it is the mark and test of our sincere concern for truth that we should be in this way open and ready to accept the falsification of our claims about how things actually are in the universe around us. By withdrawing your attention from flesh-and-blood Scots to talk of true Scotsmen, you show that your concern now is with what you would like to be, rather than what actually is, the truth.

3.21 These considerations led Popper to maintain that falsifiability is the proper criterion of demarcation between science and nonscience. It is, that is to say, an essential mark of a scientific hypothesis that it should be in principle falsifiable: that there should be intelligibly describable phenomena which, if they were to happen, would by their actual occurrence show that that hypothesis was false. A theoretical structure, like that of Isaac Newton's *Principia* (1687), which is eventually shown to have been false, is not thereby shown to have been unscientific: "We cannot identify science with truth, for we think that both Einstein's and Newton's theories belong to science, but they cannot both be true, and they may well both be false" (Popper, quoted in Magee 1973, p. 28).

3.22 What must disqualify theories or theoreticians as unscientific is rather that these theories or theoreticians refuse to allow for any things which would constitute falsifications if they were to occur. If a statement is to be substantial, then it has to deny something, something the past, present, or future occurrence of which would constitute, or would have constituted, falsification. And if a theory is to explain why this happens, then it must explain why it is this and not something else which happens. So when we learn from one of the classics of anthropology of all the many cunning intellectual devices by which the Zande ensure that no describable occurrence ever could constitute a falsification of their witchcraft beliefs, then this very discovery constitutes a sufficient reason for not awarding to this thought system the diploma title "Zande science" (Evans-Pritchard 1937, passim). Observing that Sigmund Freud (1856–1939) and his followers always seemed eager and able to show, subsequent to the event, that any and every apparently falsifying fact was after all what their own theories should have led us to expect, Popper himself contended that this constituted a very good reason for doubting whether, whatever else it may be, psychoanalysis is a science.

3.23 Either or both of these particular examples may be contested. But the general moral remains. Whenever we are uncertain, as certainly we often should be, how much, if anything, is actually being said or whether we really are being offered a genuinely explanatory and scientific theory, then we ought to press home the Falsification Challenge: "Just what, please, would have to happen, or have to have happened, to show that this statement is false or that this theory is mistaken?"

3.24 For the wife of that doomed soldier outside Stalingrad belief in God was—at least as far as the present test goes—scientific: "If there is a God ... then He will bring you back to me soon and healthy" (see paragraph 2.1). Her hypothesis was falsifiable and in fact false. It is not equally obvious that the same could be said when that original religious hypothesis is enriched, but at the same time qualified, in the fashion favored by the father of English writer Edmund Gosse (1849–1928): "Whatever you need, tell Him and He will grant it; if it is His will" (Gosse 1907, chapter 2). Fear of falsification has led many a brash, decently falsifiable hypothesis to be progressively eroded away—the death by a thousand qualifications (Flew and MacIntyre 1955, pp. 96–100).

3.25 The No-true-Scotsman Move is typically made by people who are concerned to avoid admitting that an objection brought against the truth of some proposition to which they are themselves strongly committed does indeed reveal that the proposition, at least as originally understood and maintained, is simply false. There is another somewhat similar controversial move that should be mentioned here, albeit briefly and a little distastefully. This move is typically made by people forced reluctantly to recognize deficiencies in some regime or organization or whatever else which they themselves are vehemently committed to promoting. The move is to maintain that the regime or organization or whatever else suffers from those deficiencies *only* because of some regrettable but no doubt unavoidable features of its history, and to take it that this somehow enables us to discount those reluctantly admitted deficiencies. Since this move is made as an objection to the apparently undeniable contention that the perceived deficiencies are actually present, let us introduce the label: the It-isn't-true-only-because-of-why-it-is Objection.

3.26 This objection is commonly launched against the appositeness of some stereotype, especially when the suggested explanation of its being apposite is something in the history of the human set to which it is applied which was beyond the control of members of that set. But, of course, any such explanation tacitly grants that the stereotype does indeed apply to that particular set, for thus to explain is precisely not to explain away.

3.27 Paragraph 3.26 completes the main business of chapter 3. But the chapter can be usefully and even entertainingly rounded off with a consideration of a problem originally set by Aristotle in his treatise *On Interpretation*, now conventionally referred to by its Latin title *de Interpretatione*. Aristotle's problem was to discover what, if anything, can be validly inferred from the logically necessary truth that *Either there will be a seafight tomorrow or there will not be a seafight tomorrow*. It has therefore come to be known as the Problem of the Seafight, even when the logically necessary truths being examined by Aristotle's successors contain no reference to a sea battle.

3.28 Thomas Hobbes (being English) preferred to work with a proposition about the weather. His treatment can be found in a pamphlet *Of Liberty and Necessity*. (The subtitle is too good to miss, even though it was apparently not provided by Hobbes himself but by a piratical publisher: *A Treatise wherein All Controversy Concerning Predestination, Election, Freewill, Grace, Merits, Reprobation, etc. is Fully Decided and Cleared*. Anyone seeking a more recent if less confidently definitive treatment of these questions may be referred to, for instance, Flew and Vesey 1987.) In this pamphlet Hobbes begins : "Let the case be put, for example, of the weather. It is necessary that tomorrow it shall rain or not rain. If therefore it be not necessary that it shall rain, it is necessary that it shall not rain; otherwise there is no necessity that the proposition, *It shall rain or not rain*, should be true" (emphasis original).

3.29 It should by now be obvious to us that something is going badly wrong. For here, from an empty tautological truth, Hobbes is fallaciously deducing a substantial conclusion about the (causal) necessity of the occurrence of (all) future events. The crux lies in the misplacing and consequent misinterpretation of the term "necessary." Recall that a logically necessary or necessarily true proposition is one the denial of which must involve asserting a self-contradiction. On the contrary, a logically contingent proposition is one that is logically possible, one that whether or not it happens to be true can always be denied without actual self-contradiction. The expressions "logically necessary" and "logically contingent" therefore do not belong to our ordinary, primary, first-order vocabulary for discourse about the nonlinguistic world. Instead they are elements in a vocabulary for second-order talk about talk; that is, for talk about propositions and the logical relations between propositions.

3.30 Once the difference between these two orders of discourse is noticed and its importance is appreciated, we have an excellent reason for distinguishing the propositions about which we are talking by printing them in italics. If this is done, then it is easy to see how Hobbes went wrong. For his premise now becomes: "It is a logically necessary truth that *Tomorrow it shall rain or not rain*." The logical necessity of this proposition is a consequence simply and solely of the fact that to deny it would be to contradict yourself. But the application of the same test reveals that neither the proposition *It shall rain* nor the proposition *It shall not rain* is itself a logically necessary truth. Hobbes himself was further confused by a failure to distinguish logical from physical or causal necessity. For although he certainly does not make that distinction here, he does nevertheless appear to believe that the conclusion he is entitled to draw is that whether it does or does not rain tomorrow, whatever actually does happen will have been causally necessitated.

4

Motives and Grounds

4.1 The No-true-Scotsman Move is one way in which some participants in a discussion may shift their ground, often without either those
participants themselves or any of the others involved in the discussion
clearly appreciating what is happening. There are many others. One that
is very common is the But-those-people-will-never-agree Diversion.
This is a move in which totally irrelevant bargaining considerations are
intruded into factual discussion. If one is trying to thrash out some generally acceptable working compromise on how things are to be run, then
one must consider the various sticking points of all concerned. But if
instead you are inquiring into what is in fact the case and why, then that
someone refuses to accept that this or that is true is neither here nor
there. They may be right or in error, reasonable or unreasonable, in their
refusal. But the questions which you were supposed to be discussing are
not questions about some particular person and what that person does,
or will or will not accept. Rather, they are a matter of what is actually
true, regardless of what either that particular person or anyone else may
either wish or think.

4.2 This But-those-people-will-never-agree Diversion is often executed with the help of the wretched expression "prove to." The point of

this expression, and what makes it deplorable, is to confound producing a proof with persuading a person. Yet people may be persuaded by an abominable argument just as they may remain unconvinced by considerations which they certainly would accept if only they were more rational, or more honest, or both. It may very well be that no one can prove to—that is to say persuade—Biblical Fundamentalists that our species was not specially created but was instead produced by a process of evolution through natural selection. But that is simply irrelevant to the questions of whether our species was or was not specially created, and of whether that it was or that it was not can be known to be the truth. (For some discussion of the presuppositions and implications of Darwinian theory, see, for instance, Flew 1997.)

4.3 The But-those-people-will-never-agree Diversion is one sort of move from whatever was the original subject of discussion to a different sort of question: a question about persons. Another move—let us call it the Subject/Motive Shift—is far more common. This move starts by discussing the truth or falsity of some proposition, and the grounds for holding that it has this one or that one of these alternative truth values. But it then goes on to discuss the different questions of what someone's motives might be for asserting or denying the proposition and/or for wishing to believe or to reject it. Once this distinction is clearly made, it becomes obvious that these are indeed different kinds of questions. But we still need to find ways both to keep them distinct and to pick out some of the possible connections between the two.

4.4 One reason why these two questions are so often confounded is that the word "reason" is relevantly ambiguous. When someone is said to have some reason for believing a certain proposition, we may need to ask whether this reason is a ground for holding that the proposition is actually true or whether it is a motive for persuading oneself of it, irrespective of whether it is true or not. In the former case we can speak either of a reason (ground) or of an evidencing reason, in the latter either of a reason (motive) or of a motivating reason. We might also distinguish a third sense of "reason." For instance, in the phrase "one reason why" at the beginning of the present paragraph, what is being referred to is neither of the first two sorts of reason but rather a cause.

4.5 The classic occasion for distinguishing the first two of these three senses of "reason" is provided by the famous argument known as Pascal's Wager. Others have urged that the existence of a universe that exhibits certain special characteristics constitutes evidence for, or even proof of, the existence of some kind of God. There is, for instance, what is known as the Argument from, or, better, the Argument to, Design. But in his *Pensées* the philosopher-mathematician Blaise Pascal (1623–1662) begins by conceding that there are no grounds, no evidences, adequate to warrant the desired conclusion: "Reason can decide nothing here." Pascal maintains that we are all confronted by a situation in which it is inescapably compulsory to make a bet. He sees only two possible ways to bet and insists that no one has any alternative but to stake his or her life in one or the other of these two ways. The one bet is that the teachings of Roman Catholicism are true. If you bet this way you become or, as the case may be, remain a believing and practicing Roman Catholic. The other bet is that those teachings are false. If you bet that way you reject Roman Catholicism and you live your life on the assumption that your death will be your annihilation.

4.6 In terms of the present distinction between senses of the word "reason," what Pascal was saying was that, although we have no sufficient reasons (grounds) for believing that the teachings of Roman Catholicism are true, we do have the very best of reasons (motives) for trying to persuade ourselves that they are. For if they are true and we bet our lives on the truth, then we stand to make the infinite gain of Heaven. But if they are false and we had bet our lives on their being true, then our loss in leading Roman Catholic lives—even if we do persist in seeing that as a loss—will at worst have been strictly finite. Suppose, however, that we bet our lives on the secular alternative. If we were right to reject Roman Catholic teachings as false, then it is our gains which turn out to have been finite, which we always believed they would be. But if we were wrong, then it is our loss which will be infinite, an eternity of the most extreme tortures in Hell. It is therefore clear that, always given Pascal's assumptions, he is right to conclude that anyone would be mad to make their bet in any sense other than that which he recommends. (For a critique of this Wager argument see, for instance, Flew 1984, chapter 5.)

4.7 The further distinction between reasons (grounds) and reasons (causes) becomes essential if we want even to begin adequately to critique an argument such as the following: "In deriving mind and knowledge from nature, as science conceives it, 'the naturalist' must assume that his own account of nature is true. But on his premises, the truth of this account, like that of any other bit of knowledge, is merely the function of the adjustment of the organism to its environment. . . . This entire conception of knowledge refutes itself" (Urban 1949, p. 236).

4.8 W. R. Urban, like so many other writers, is, in effect, arguing that if there are always physiological reasons why I utter the sounds which I do utter, then I cannot have, and know that I have, good reasons for believing the propositions which I assert by uttering those sounds. If it is the one, then it must be merely that and not the other. But now, in terms of our further distinction, the physiological reasons must be reasons (causes), whereas the good reasons which I may or may not have for believing can only be reasons (grounds). So no reason (ground) has been given why "reasons," in these two different senses of "reason," should be considered as necessarily rivals for the same space, with the presence of one precluding that of the other. (For a thorough examination of an argument of this kind, as C. S. Lewis presented it in the first edition of his *Miracles*, see Anscombe 1981, chapter 21.)

4.9 A first general lesson of method for us to draw from the previous five paragraphs is that wherever we need to distinguish two or more senses of a word, there we also need to supply informative parentheses in order to maintain the distinctions made. The model to imitate, which I have been imitating, is that of funny (ha ha) as popularly and correctly distinguished from funny (peculiar). For even after an ambiguity has apparently been recognized, the temptation is to plunge on as if the crucial distinction had never been made. Thus, while claiming to have accepted the distinctions indicated earlier (see paragraph 4.4), someone may nevertheless continue to argue just as before that if the reason why I believe something is physiological, then I cannot have any sufficient reason for believing it. But it would scarcely be possible for anyone to do this if he or she had shown, by inserting the appropriate parentheses, that he or she had really recognized the ambiguity.

4.10 A second lesson will perhaps only be completely mastered when we work—as here—with engagingly important and tricky examples. It can be hard to come fully to terms with the fact that a word may be entirely ambiguous, with senses as different and as unconnected logically as those of any two wholly different and etymologically unrelated words. For example, in chapter 1 we had occasion to distinguish two radically different senses of the word "democracy" (see paragraph 1.30).

4.11 In one of these two senses—call it liberal—an institution is democratic to the extent that it is in due season possible for its members to vote the leadership out, if that is what those members want to do. In the other sense—call it paternalist—an institution is democratic to the extent that it serves the true needs and interests of its rank-and-file members, usually as determined by some particular elite individual or set of individuals. Given this distinction, it becomes tempting to speak of two varieties or species of democracy—especially if you yourself happen to want to appropriate for one of these supposed varieties or species favorable attitudes originally directed toward the other. But our word "democracy" derives from Greek words meaning people power, and it has retained this primary meaning in English. So democracy (paternalist) is the very opposite, rather than another variety, of democracy (liberal).

4.12 The reason why mistakes of the kind discussed in the previous three paragraphs are so tempting—the cause of the trouble, that is—is that speech habits are just as much habits as any others and just as hard to form or to break. Maintaining a distinction between two senses of a word requires that some entrenched habits of association be overcome and that others be formed. The least one can do is to make suitable parenthetical insertions whenever we employ the ambiguous word in any possibly troublesome context. In this way the desired associations of what is inserted pull against the undesired associations of the ambiguous term. In the exceptionally intractable case, where this routine treatment proves ineffective, the ambiguous term should be jettisoned completely and replaced by two words or expressions that do not look alike and so do not have the same associations.

4.13 The most common, indeed the most dully commonplace, case of the Subject/Motive Shift is that in which an assertion is dismissed as false or an argument is discredited as unsound for no other and better reason than that it is made or presented by an interested party. Certainly it is right always to be alert to the possibility that assertions and arguments are being corrupted by the self-interests of the asserters and the arguers. And there is little need to warn most of us to be alert to the possibility that the statements and arguments of businesspersons, politicians, labor-union spokespersons, and public-relations officers may be corrupted by various forms of self-interest. Everyone, too, knows the cynic's definition of ambassadors as people sent abroad to lie for their countries.

4.14 It may very well be that as an ambassador, labor-union official, or public-relations officer, he or she is paid to say a certain thing or argue in a certain way. But that material interest by itself does not constitute good or even any grounds for concluding that those representatives' claims must be false and their arguments must be invalid. Those of us who do not belong to any of these three suspect classes often present sound arguments for conclusions that happen to be both true and to our advantage. The truth is no more necessarily disagreeable than it is necessarily agreeable.

4.15 No one is likely to want to deny outright anything asserted in the two previous paragraphs. The problem is, as with many other important truisms, to discipline ourselves so that we are never carried away by the heat of the moment. We must always remember that even a truism may be true. One step in the right direction might be for everyone to collect his or her own sets of arresting examples. Such sets need to be individually collected and individually weighted to offset each individual's particular assemblage of biases. For instance, if someone is generally inclined to suspect the truthfulness of businessmen or diplomats or labor spokespersons, then that person's collection of examples has to contain statements from members of these particular, notoriously sinister, occupational groups, statements which, when made, have been contemptuously disbelieved by that person and by other opponents, but which nevertheless turned out to have contained the truth and nothing but the truth.

4.16 Notwithstanding the recent development of the economics of public choice, however, many people apparently remain unaware of the very real and live possibility of corruptions resulting from the private interests of employees of public and semipublic organizations, corruptions resulting from their private interests precisely as employees of those particular organizations. Employees of agencies established to combat perceived evils, for instance, cannot but have strong job-preservation interests in the continuation of at least sufficient of those evils to justify the preservation of the agency which employs them. If and insofar as those evils are indeed diminished, either by the activities of the agencies themselves or by independent technological and social developments, it becomes necessary, just to maintain present levels of employment and funding, for those agencies somehow to identify further supposed examples of the evils in question. (For a brief account of the nature of the economics of public choice, consult the preface to Buchanan 1991. The classic contribution to that area of economics is Buchanan and Tullock 1962.)

4.17 This is certainly no place for a general investigation of the ways in which such possibilities have in fact frequently been realized: for instance, in the Equal Employment Opportunities Commission (EEOC) and the Environmental Protection Agency (EPA) in the United States or in similar organizations in other countries. But it is for us very relevant to refer to a case in which the identification of an abundance of further supposed examples of the evils in question is achieved by tacitly transforming the meaning of the key word; the word, that is to say, used to refer to that evil.

4.18 For example, the EEOC does this when it discovers what it calls indirect discrimination to have occurred when some minority subset of the total national population is found not to be proportionately represented either in some kind of employment in some particular geographical area or among those employed by a single employer throughout the country. The employers concerned are then presumed, until and unless they are able to prove their innocence, to have been guilty of hostile discrimination against members of the minority subset in question. It is notoriously hard to prove a negative. So, paradoxically, the only sure way for employers to provide acceptable proof that they were innocent of hostile discrimination against members of some minority subset is for them to operate a quota policy of positive preferential discrimination in favor of members of that minority subset. Presumably the EEOC recognized that discrimination as a kind of choosing is essentially intentional. This was no doubt part of the reason why the EEOC decided that what it was proposing to combat as a supposed further form of the evil of discrimination must be described not as unintended but as indirect discrimination.

4.19 The economist Lester Thurow, however, on the second page of his *Poverty and Discrimination* (1969) simply defines "discrimination" as his word for all the actual differences with respect to economic prospects and economic achievements among members of the various sets which he there chooses to distinguish. This is done altogether without any reference to causes from which these differences may have resulted. Thurow then proceeds to provide an abundance of statistics showing the extent of these differences, a proceeding which, according to his definition, constitutes the provision of statistics showing the extent of discrimination. All intergroup differences in cultural orientation toward education, work, family, risk, self-employment, enterprise, and everything else have been banished from consideration by definition. "Discrimination" here becomes a word for nothing but statistical results, although the very reason why most of us are concerned about discrimination in the usual understanding of that word is that, in that understanding, it refers to a particular and unlovely kind of intentional behavior.

4.20 By this verbal maneuver Thurow not only abandons inquiry into the causes of these observed and recorded intergroup differences, causes of which hostile or favorable (direct) discrimination is certainly only one cause although perhaps in certain cases the most important cause. At the same time, he attempts to redirect the moral disapproval of his readers from such discrimination as a possible cause of these intergroup differences to the intergroup differences as such. In so doing he appears to be trying to persuade us to abandon the ideal of equality of opportunity, which forbids discrimination upon grounds which are properly irrelevant, and to abandon it in favor of the very different, and in practice incompatible, ideal of equality of outcome.

4.21 Thurow presents this altogether different ideal of equality of outcome in an oblique and very misleading way, as if its realization could be achieved by systematically preventing all defections from the entirely different ideal of nondiscriminatory equality of opportunity. Thurow, like everyone else, is fully entitled, if he so wishes, to proclaim his personal ideals straightforwardly, and to endeavor to persuade others to join him in pursuing those ideals. But to present what appears to be his own personal ideal as if it were a very different ideal, and that one which is today almost universally shared, that is a different matter. (For some discussion of the relations or lack of relations between these two different ideals of equality see, for instance, Flew 1981, chapter 2.)

4.22 Paragraphs 4.13–4.14 brought out that the Subject/Motive Shift is fallacious, whereas paragraph 4.15 suggested a salutary disciplinary drill. The Subject/Motive Shift now needs to be distinguished from three other moves that are perfectly proper and on occasion absolutely necessary. Certainly it is fallacious to urge that simply because someone has a vested interest in the truth of a proposition or in the validity of an argument, the proposition or argument is, or very probably is, therefore, false or, as the case may be, invalid.

4.23 But in the first place suppose that the proposition has been asserted by someone giving evidence in a court. It remains always relevant that a particular proposition may be both true and known by the person who asserts it, notwithstanding that the person has every kind of powerful vested interest in both its truth and the assertion of its truth. But that it is asserted by someone who is in a position to know and has no reason (motive) for trying to deceive us, is for us, who are not in that person's position to know, better evidence for believing that it is true than the same assertion made by someone in an equally good position to know, but with opposite interests. There are, of course, other dimensions of complexity in the reasonable assessment of testimony. The present point is, however, simple and uncontroversial. For instance, it is taken for granted by everyone who in a question of foul play would be inclined, all other things being equal, to accept the testimony of a neutral spectator rather than that of any of the contestants.

4.24 The second entirely legitimate kind of move which needs to be distinguished from the fallacious Subject/Motive Shift is what I call the On-your-own-principles Maneuver. It is entirely legitimate and perfectly proper to point out to opponents in argument logical consequences of their own contentions; in doing this one does not necessarily commit oneself to either accepting or rejecting those contentions. Indeed, this is the typical form of rational moral argument. For if one wants to persuade people rationally to alter or abandon what they hold as their moral principles, how else could this be done save by revealing to them logical consequences of those principles which they themselves are not prepared to accept as moral? (For further discussion of the nature of rational moral argument see, for instance, R. M. Hare 1952; and compare paragraphs 5.41–5.46, below.)

4.25 People against whom this On-your-own-principles Maneuver is employed may be tempted to complain that its employment constitutes an illicit *argumentum ad hominem*. This Latin expression means, literally, an argument addressed to the man. It is an expression we need to understand but ought never to employ ourselves. For a start it is unacceptably sexist. But, much more the present point, it is an expression that has been and still is regularly employed to refer not only to a kind of fallacy, but also to a sort of argument which is perfectly proper. The fallacy in question may be seen as a variant of the Subject/Motive Shift. The premise attributes some discreditable characteristic to the other party in the argument, whereas the conclusion purports thereby to establish the falsity of some thesis propounded by that party. The perfectly proper form of argument is that of executing the On-your-own-principles Maneuver.

4.26 It cannot be too often or too strongly emphasized that those who execute this maneuver are not thereby and necessarily committing themselves to the actual or pretended principles of those against whom they perform it. To emphasize this is indeed the main point and purpose of refusing to speak of *ad hominem* arguments and introducing instead the expression "On-your-own-Principles Maneuver." For example, suppose that some set of politicians were found to have been profiting hugely from deals of a kind which they had themselves repeatedly and loudly denounced as utterly illicit. And suppose that opponents then pointed to the inconsistency between the actual behavior of that set of politicians and their own frequently stated principles. Then it would be preposterous for these politicians to respond by claiming that since their opponents themselves were well known to have benefited as much or more by making the same kind of deals, they were just as hypocritical. For we are assuming that those opponents had never maintained that such deals are wrong and had never pretended not to be making them.

4.27 There is a third perfectly legitimate move which needs to be distinguished from the fallacious Subject/Motive Shift. There is one condition on which it is entirely legitimate to raise and to pursue questions about interests and motivations. If and only if the original questions of truth and validity have been settled, then—at least from the point of view of soundness of thinking—it is perfectly legitimate and it can often be very illuminating to raise and pursue such questions. For, given that some individual or some set of individuals is mistaken and now known to be mistaken, and given that we have no evidencing reason to believe that individual or set of individuals to be in general intellectually challenged, then we may reasonably expect to discover what it is which is misleading that person or set of people. Yet it will not do—notwithstanding that it is all too often done—to offer more or less speculative answers to such consequential questions as a substitute for, rather than as a supplement to, the direct examination of whatever were the prior issues.

4.28 It appears that this offense is more prevalent today than ever before. Certainly the temptation has been much increased by the proliferation of psychoanalysis and the sociology of knowledge. Consider a statement by a leading British Freudian, Charles Berg: "To achieve success the analyst must above all be an analyst. That is to say he must know positively that all human emotional reactions, all human judgments, and even reason itself, are nothing but the tools of the unconscious; that such seemingly acute convictions which an intelligent person like this possesses are but the inevitable effect of causes which lie buried within the unconscious levels of his psyche" (Berg 1946, p. 190).

4.29 Suppose that the scope of this statement had been explicitly limited to the analytic situation and that its application had been emphatically confined to neurotic patients crying out for psychiatric attention. Still, many lay readers would have inferred that psychoanalysis licenses the absolutely general conclusion "that all human emotional reactions, all human judgments, and even reason itself, are nothing but the tools of the unconscious" (Berg 1946, p. 190). As it is, Dr. Berg was apparently presenting this reckless and unqualified claim as either a finding or a presupposition of psychoanalytic investigations. For what else could be the point of his saying that this is something which the successful analyst "must know positively"? Presumably some rule of professional procedure (i.e., never to attend to the truth or validity value of anything the client says in the analytic hour but always to seek some motive for the client's saying it) is being confused with, and mistaken to warrant, the conclusion that such utterances—and hence by a somewhat drastic extension all utterances (presumably including the utterances of psychoanalysts reporting what they believe to be their own findings)—do not actually have, and/or cannot be known actually to have, any truth or validity value at all. Nothing like leather becomes, not for the first nor for the only time, nothing but leather.

4.30 Be that as it may with these interpretative conjectures, there is no doubt but that, if psychoanalysis really does carry any such universal consequence, then the entire enterprise must thereby discredit itself. For this is exactly that same disastrous consequence which, as we saw earlier (see paragraphs 4.7–4.8), has often, but wrongly, been said to be implicit in any form of scientific "naturalism." Let us put this objection in the most pointed and personal way. If "all human judgments . . . are nothing but the tools of the unconscious," and if the point of this "nothing but" is, as it surely must be, to preclude the possibility of these tools of the unconscious also being known to be true, then this must apply equally to all the judgments of the no-more-than-human analyst, and hence that "all" has to include the judgment which the psychoanalyst himself is here making about all human judgments. What is poison for the goose is poison for the gander (and for the farmer, too).

4.31 It is therefore understandable, if not on that account venial, that usually those who see the putative insights of psychoanalysis as instruments for discrediting opinions apply these instruments only to other people. To lose the initiative would be fatal. It thus has to be the opinions of other people rather than our own that are, with no good grounds given, dismissed as nothing but the expressions of unconscious motivation. Thus, it has to be the motives of other people rather than our own to which the Subject/Motive Shift shifts.

4.32 With appropriate alterations what has just been said also applied to Marxist sociologists of knowledge and still applies if there are still Marxist sociologists of knowledge to whom anything can apply. It had, and perhaps has, to be the opinions of other people that were as such repudiated as nothing but the "false consciousness" of a particular social or economic class. The pretended findings of these Marxists naturally were not in the same way mere ideology, but instead science, perhaps even "scientific socialism." A similar, more recently fashionable contention, is that of the Deconstructionists. Since in their view all knowledge is socially constructed, books (i.e., texts) are interesting only for revealing their author's ideology rather than for their apparent content. This contention therefore generates the ideally appropriate rule for interpreting the writings of Deconstructionists themselves, if anyone should think it worthwhile to spend time in this fashion.

4.33 For anyone who sincerely wants to know what's what, the right moral to draw from these proceedings is that whatever relevant insights psychoanalysis and sociology may be alleged to give us should be applied in the first instance rather than as a last resort to ourselves. It is most salutary to remember and to follow an example set by Charles Darwin. Long before Freud was even born Darwin made it his practice to note down all objections to his theories the moment he met them. That observant naturalist had noticed that we are all more apt to forget what we have some interest in not remembering.

4.34 Another common move which resembles the Subject/Motive Shift is not the same, although it too is unsound. Someone ripostes to a speaker who has put forward a view that is distinctively Christian, Marxist, Conservative, or whatever: "You would believe that because you are a Christian (or a Marxist, or a Conservative, or a whatever)." Such remarks may often have point and value. But they cannot be admitted as objections. For that some view happens to be an essential element in some general position only begins to be relevant to the question of the truth of that particular view when the general position is already known to be in error. But to appeal to this assumption of error in a debate with someone who starts as an adherent of that particular general position constitutes a textbook example of Begging the Question, that is, of taking for granted precisely what is in dispute. Furthermore, even if the general Christian, Marxist, Conservative, or whatever position is in error, it could—and almost certainly does—contain some elements and carry some consequences which are in their own right true.

4.35 Such attempts to refute a view merely by classifying it in some irrelevant way are not the same as attempts to refute a view by referring to the possible motives of its protagonists. One favorite contemporary token of the former type (see paragraph 1.49) is to meet a contention by dismissing it on no other or better ground than that it is well worn, hackneyed, boring, or predictable. It ought to go without saying that none of these facts, even if it is indeed a fact, has by itself any bearing at all upon the question of the truth value of the proposition so characterized. It is a scandal of our trendocratic times that a purely journalistic classification of this kind should so often be allowed to pass as a refutation.

4.36 Another token of the same type was common in the United States during the Vietnam War. Some said that if South Vietnam were to be allowed to fall to the Communists, then Laos, Cambodia, and other countries of Southeast Asia would follow in quick succession. Their position was regularly described as the Domino Theory. Yet the very aptness of this happy description was almost equally regularly mistaken to be a disproof of that theory. Certainly almost everyone at that time whom I challenged to give evidencing reasons for dismissing that theory seemed surprised to be so challenged. Most apparently believed that the description was itself sufficient refutation. So let us do our bit to discourage bad practice by introducing a suitably opprobrious label: the Fallacy of Pseudorefuting Description.

4.37 Today this fallacy is perhaps most commonly committed by peremptorily dismissing hopefully explanatory accounts of human events as conspiracy theories. That is clearly not an adequate, or indeed any, refutation. But in investigating the actual outcomes of social and political policies we do need to be aware that these policies always do in fact have consequences which were unforeseen and hence unintended by the promoters of those policies. This is why the social sciences have sometimes been defined as studies of the unintended consequences of intended action. Once we have recognized that it is possible, even likely, that policies may have consequences which were not intended by the promoters of those policies, we ought at least to hesitate and seek clearer evidence before accusing them of conspiring to produce those consequences. (For some discussion of the special difficulties of discussing social facts and social policies see, for instance, Flew

1995. Murray 1984, although by now somewhat dated, is still a book which should be read by anyone who wants to engage in critical thinking about the United States or any similar welfare system.)

4.38 This is the moment to say something about the cry: "We want no witch-hunts." Certainly there are two reasons, each of which is by itself more than sufficient, for not wanting to see a revival of that ancient and fortunately now long-since-defunct institution. One is that in truth there neither have been nor could be women either naturally endowed with nor able to acquire the powers to do the deeds witches were believed to do. The other is that the hunt for victims allegedly guilty of doing such deeds typically, if perhaps not quite universally, involved the use of torture to extract confessions. (For a historian's account of the horrors of such actual witch-hunts, consult Trevor-Roper 1956.)

4.39 Since, at least in the Western world, no one in our time believes that there are or could be people actually endowed with the powers the victims of historic witch-hunts were accused of exercising, no one today can be honestly and truthfully accused of being in that sense a witch. So if and when any of our contemporaries are accused of advocating or conducting a witch-hunt, their first response to their accusers should be to ask those accusers what they see as the analogies between whatever it is which the accused are advocating or themselves doing and the witch-hunts of history.

4.40 The closest actual analogue to a witch-hunt in the twentieth century would seem to have been the great terror launched by J. V. Stalin in the mid-1930s. But in that terror the most prominent victims were tortured into confessing to have committed offenses that were at least physically possible for human beings to have committed. In that case, on the other hand, those who ordered the torturing, and probably many of the torturers themselves, knew that those prominent victims had not in truth committed the offenses to which they were required to confess. (For the most comprehensive account of this great terror, revised in the light of evidence which has become available only since the collapse of the USSR, see Conquest 1992.)

5

Minding Our Language

5.1 The Fallacy of Pseudorefuting Description is essentially obscurantist. For the effect, and too often the object, of committing this fallacy is to dismiss blindly and with no evidencing reasons given whatever is so described. Today this fallacy is perhaps most commonly committed by describing someone's beliefs about what is or is not the case as racist, and dismissing those beliefs from further consideration on that account alone. Here, as has been suggested earlier (see paragraphs 1.44–1.47), the crucial and too often unmade distinction is the one between, on the one hand, beliefs about what is or is not the case and, on the other hand, a kind of behavior, or, in the present case, misbehavior. When someone's behavior is truly described as racist, it is inasmuch as the person has discriminated either in favor of or against individual members of some particular racially defined set for no other or better reason (on no other or better ground) than that those fortunate or, as the case may be, unfortunate individuals were members of that particular racially defined set. Such behavior is obviously unfair and on that account deplorable.

5.2 But suppose someone is condemned as a racist not for any such deplorable behavior but for his or her beliefs about what actually is or is not the case. For example, suppose that he or she has found evidencing reason to doubt, and has expressed their disbelief in, some of the implications of a remarkably comprehensive and categorical pronouncement issued in 1965 by the U.S. Department of Labor, a pronouncement issued on its own sheer authority and without the citation of any supporting evidence. This read: "Intelligence potential is distributed among Negro infants in the same proportion and pattern as among Icelanders or Chinese, or any other group. . . . There is absolutely no question of any genetic differential."

5.3 But anyone who is condemned as a racist for no other or better reason than that he or she does not accept and has expressed disbelief concerning some of the implications of this departmental pronouncement is in effect being condemned as a heretic; a person, that is to say, who rejects some of the established and approved beliefs of a society of which he or she is a member. But the liberal and civilized way to deal with the propounders of heresies is not to make them outcasts but to try to refute their heresies (see paragraphs 1.57–1.58). Providing only and always that the heretical beliefs were the outcomes of open-minded and sincerely truth-seeking inquiry, heretics surely cannot be blamed for holding their no doubt erroneous beliefs?

5.4 In the three previous paragraphs I was taking it for granted that the allegedly racist beliefs are beliefs not about all members of particular racial sets but only about averages across those sets. All the allegedly racist beliefs that various psychologists, biologists, and social scientists have in recent years been denounced and hounded for holding and expressing have been of this statistical kind. These beliefs, therefore, provided no rational basis for discrimination either in favor of or against any particular individual member of any of the racial sets in question. For example, as stated earlier, from a proposition stating the average height of all the members of some set one cannot validly infer the height of any individual member of that set. The situation would be different if anyone claimed that members of some racial set either all possessed or all lacked some characteristic needed in many sorts of employment and achievement. But such a manifestly false belief could scarcely be the outcome of open-minded and sincerely truth-seeking inquiry.

5.5 Committing the Fallacy of Pseudorefuting Description is one way of disposing of disfavored assertions without undertaking the perhaps unachievable labor of refutation. Another more comprehensive way is to develop a systematic vocabulary on the lines of the "Newspeak" of George Orwell's last appalling nightmare *1984* (1949). This once very widely known novel is probably little read since the collapse of the Union of Soviet Socialist Republics (USSR), the emancipation of its satellite "People's Democracies," and the consequent end of the Cold War. For *1984* was written in 1948. It presents the author's vision of life thirty-six years later in an England that has become a part of one of three global empires: Eurasia, Eastasia, and Oceana.

5.6 Oceana, the largest of these empires, is ruled in a manner which Orwell saw as similar to J. V. Stalin's rule in and over the USSR. In the book Oceana is developing a new artificial language in hopes that this will finally replace "Oldspeak (or Standard English, as we should call it) by about the year 2050" (p. 305). The aim, as Orwell went on to explain in his appendix on the principles of Newspeak, was "to meet the ideological needs of Ingsoc, or English Socialism. . . . Newspeak was not only to provide a medium of expression for the world-view and mental habits proper to the devotees of Ingsoc, but to make all other modes of thought impossible. . . . Newspeak was designed not to extend but to diminish the range of thought, and this purpose was indirectly assisted by cutting the choice of words down to a minimum" (pp. 305–306). Orwell quotes the well-known passage from the American Declaration of Independence beginning: "We hold these truths to be self-evident, that all men are created equal, that they are endowed by their Creator with certain unalienable rights . . ." (pp. 317–18). The whole passage could in Newspeak be rendered only as "doubleplus ungood crimethink" (p. 318)—an impoverishing misrepresentation that carries with it a simultaneous and wholly prejudicial shudder of rejection (see paragraph 1.59).

5.7 Orwell's concern with language as the main vehicle of thought and his commitment to struggle against all the tendencies that the inventors of Newspeak labored to promote can also be seen in his splendid essay on "Politics and the English Language" (in Orwell 1968). In it he picks out and pillories empty phrases and dead metaphors which do not so much express as conceal thought—or the lack of it. Above all he assails such euphemistic abstractions as "the elimination of unreliable elements," abstractions that are both introduced and employed in order to distract attention from the cruelties and the injustices to which they refer.

5.8 Orwell's concern in that essay is not the same as concern for and commitment to euphony and literary elegance. Both concerns are often found together—in Orwell himself, for instance. But any preference that any conservative English person may have for the Old World monosyllable "lift," as opposed to its less terse transatlantic equivalent "elevator" is, when we are thinking about thinking, neither here nor there. What by contrast has to be relevant is any usage or abusage that tends either to reduce the stock of concepts available or to conceal the meaning of what is supposed to be being said.

5.9 I suppose in a philistine moment we might dismiss issues of the former kind as merely or trivially verbal. But if these are to be our paradigms of the merely verbal, then it becomes preposterous to condemn upon the same grounds questions of the second kind, too. For the nub of the distinction between these two different sorts of issue about words precisely is that the one refers only to possible forms of expression and not to the content of what might be said, whereas the other is concerned essentially with the meanings that are or might be expressed. The question of whether we should say "He got in touch with her" rather than "He contacted her" is indeed trivially verbal. But the question of whether we should say "He did kill him" rather than "He did not kill him" is, notwithstanding that it can be represented as a matter of whether or not to insert one particular three-letter word, a matter of substance. In the most literal sense it happens to be a question of life and death.

5.10 Therefore, although witty, it was unfair of Edward Gibbon (1737–1794), the author of the famous history of *The Decline and Fall of the Roman Empire*, to ridicule the Christian world for splitting over an iota. For the fact that the dispute between those contending that the Son is of like substance (in Greek, *homoiousios*) and those maintaining that He is of the same substance (in Greek, *homoousios*) as the Father can be represented as a dispute over the insertion or excision of one Greek letter is a wretched reason for suggesting that any difference so symbolized must be correspondingly insignificant. It is none of our present business to decide whether this particular conclusion happens to be true or whether the great conflict centered on a distinction without a

difference or whether it all was in some other way misguided or gratu-
itous. For us, the point is simply that Gibbon's witticism provides no
support whatever for any such conclusion.

5.11 From the beginning of chapter 1 I have been pointing out that
and why, if we want to think better and straighter, we have to school ourselves to follow stricter and perhaps less common usages of certain crucial terms: "valid" and "invalid," for instance, as well as "true" and
"false," "know" and "refute," and "prejudice." Orwell, in "Politics and
the English Language," extends this concern about language to include
style and syntax as well as vocabulary: "People are imprisoned for years
without trial, or shot in the back of the neck, or sent to die of scurvy in
Arctic lumber camps: this is called 'elimination of unreliable elements'.
. . . The inflated style is itself a kind of euphemism. A mass of Latin
words falls upon the facts like soft snow, blurring the outlines and cov-
ering up all the details. The great enemy of clear language is insincerity.
When there is a gap between one's real and one's declared aims, one
turns as it were instinctively to long words and exhausted idioms, like a
cuttlefish squirting out ink" (Vol. IV, pp. 166–67).

5.12 Fuller development of the theme that some improvements of our
style are necessary to the improvement of our thought I must leave to others,
above all to Orwell himself. It is enough here to have said that this is so and
to have insisted that this kind of concern about language is not to be dismissed as trivially verbal, whereas another kind of concern might be considered to be so. Orwell also suggests that the call for clear, brief, careful,
concrete, and down-to-earth expression is a call for integrity, a call for hon-
esty both to oneself and to other people. So let us note two of the maxims of
that great French aphorist, the Marquis de Vauvenargues: "Obscurity is the
kingdom of error" and "For the philosopher clarity is a matter of good faith."

5.13 Vagueness, too, can be a fault. The first thing to notice about
vagueness is that it ought not to be, although it often is, equated with
ambiguity. To say of some word or expression or of some whole statement
that it is ambiguous is to say that it can be construed in at least two different ways. (See, for instance, paragraphs 1.14–1.15 and 4.4–4.12.)
Anyone who says this asks for, and should be ready to meet, the challenge: What two interpretations do you want to distinguish?

5.14 To complain of vagueness is to complain that what has been said is unacceptably indeterminate in some relevant dimension. To promise to stop by during the afternoon is to make a less precise commitment than to promise to arrive between four and six o'clock. Neither the more vague nor the more precise of these alternative promises is in any obvious way ambiguous. Equally a person may call something ambiguous without either of its alternative interpretations being such as to expose that person to the charge of imprecision. Suppose, however, that you ask me: "How did you expect them to behave?" Then your question will be importantly ambiguous. For it might reasonably be construed as an inquiry: either about what I had believed that they would in fact do; or about what I had considered that they ought to have done. Yet in neither of these different interpretations would your question have been in any obvious way vague or imprecise. Since this ambiguity of the word "expect" is one we need to keep in mind, I must follow some of my own advice (see paragraph 4.9). Let the first of the two senses just distinguished be labeled descriptive and the second prescriptive.

5.15 The second thing to notice about vagueness is that it is not a fault in a language that it provides, or provides for, some words and expressions that are more vague than others. It is reasonable to complain only when and insofar as "what has been said is unacceptably indeterminate in some relevant dimension." Suppose that I am in no position to say more about my time of arrival than that it will be during the afternoon. Then it must be unjust to condemn me for not specifying closer limits, and it would be an awkward defect, not a merit, in my language if it rendered me unable to say the only thing I was entitled to assert. The traditional stock example of a vague term is the word "bald." No doubt we could so redefine this word that in its future correct usage it implied some specific density of, or some specific total, hair population. But this would be a silly move. For we should be exchanging a humbly serviceable tool, which we often have occasion to employ, for a shiny new piece of futile equipment, which in our normal everyday life we never should be in a position to use correctly.

5.16 Vagueness, insofar as it is a matter of "what has been said" being unacceptably indeterminate "in some relevant dimension," must be a bad thing. But whether or not some particular measure of indeterminacy is in some particular context culpable, we have to notice a third general point. It is that any indeterminacy in the premises of an argument is bound to infect whatever conclusions can be validly deduced from these premises with a precisely corresponding indeterminacy. Given appropriate alterations, exactly the same applies when it is a question of unreliability in the premises. That these things must be so follows from the essential nature of a valid deductive argument (see paragraph 1.10). Since to deny the conclusions of such an argument while nevertheless affirming its premises would be to contradict oneself, these conclusions must be implicitly or explicitly contained in those premises. It is therefore impossible to get more or better than you put in at the outset. The situation is the same as that epitomized in slogans once popular among hard-bitten computer buffs: "Garbage produces garbage!" or, better, "Garbage in, garbage out (GIGO)!"

5.17 The fourth point to be made about vagueness is that if you choose to redefine some vague term in such a way that it becomes in the usage thus stipulated more precise, then you will have given another and different meaning to that word: "To remove vagueness is to outline the penumbra of a shadow. The line is there after we have drawn it, but not before."

5.18 Ambiguity may be innocuous. Surely little harm has ever come from the ambiguity of the word "bank"? In one sense a bank is that whereon, if both passersby and various public authorities permit, Shakespeare's wild thyme blows. In the other a bank is what looks after your money and may or not be eager to lend you some of its own. Sometimes too ambiguities may be exploited in a way which is useful and perfectly straightforward.

5.19 Consider, for instance, an ambiguous term like "expect," in which the two meanings, though different, are not logically incompatible. It therefore becomes possible for the leaders of organizations to announce in a single sentence not including any conjunction their expectations both that something ought to happen and that it will happen. By that very announcement they may hope to make it more likely that their expectation that the thing will happen will in the event not be disappointed. For English people the best-known example of such a deliberately and pointedly ambiguous announcement was the signal the charismatic English commanding Admiral Horatio Nelson ordered to be hoisted as his ships began to engage in the great decisive naval battle of the Napoleonic wars: "England expects every man to do his duty."

5.20 Ambiguity becomes seriously confusing only where both interpretations of the ambiguous word or expression are relevant in the same context and where those two interpretations are in that context in some way in conflict. For example, consider the expression "religious knowledge." It is employed in both weak and strong senses. In the former sense it refers to knowledge about the religious beliefs people actually hold and the religious practices those beliefs require and support, but without any implications either about the truth or falsity of these religious beliefs or about the propriety of the practices they support. In the latter sense the expression "religious knowledge" carries the implications that the religious beliefs in question constitute items of knowledge and that the associated practices are properly imperative.

5.21 There are two frequently realized dangers here. One is that those who have failed to observe this crucial distinction will mistake it that considerations sufficient to justify the teaching of religious knowledge in the weak sense must also, by the same token, be sufficient to justify its teaching in the strong sense. The other danger is that those who believe that there is no such thing as religious knowledge (strong sense) may fail to recognize the possibility of religious knowledge (weak sense) and hence fail to appreciate that there may nevertheless be a strong case for teaching children some items of that knowledge in their schools.

5.22 For another example of an important and often overlooked ambiguity consider *An Approach to Social Policy* (1975), an official document of the National Economic and Social Council (NESC) of the Republic of Ireland published by the Stationery Office in Dublin. From this document we discover that the NESC is by its terms of reference required to "promote social justice." Such promotion apparently either involves or simply is "the fair and equitable distribution of the income and wealth of the nation."

5.23 But expressions such as "the income and wealth of the nation," "the national wealth," "Gross Domestic Product" (GDP), and "Gross National Product" (GNP) are all systematically misleading because they systematically confound the sums of the income or the wealth of all the individual citizens and of all the privately owned firms in a nation-state with the amounts of income collectively acquired and wealth collectively owned by that state as such. Except in socialist states, in which all or almost all productive equipment is owned by the state itself, sums of the former kind are bound to be very much larger than sums of the latter sort.

5.24 In this understanding of the meaning of the word "socialism" nearly all presently existing states either already are or are in the process of becoming nonsocialist states. Therefore, if in such a state it is thought that the actual distribution of wealth and income is not "fair and acceptable," then what is here described as *social justice* apparently requires that some of what we must, albeit defeasibly, presume to have been the justly acquired income and wealth of those considered to get and to have more than is "fair and equitable" must be compulsorily extracted from them by the state in order to transfer it—less, inevitably, some handling charge—to others who have not previously succeeded in justly acquiring and retaining the amounts which it is considered to be "fair and equitable" for them to acquire and to have. Because the author of that Irish report failed to make the crucial distinction between the two senses of such expressions as "the national income" he also failed to notice how very far removed what is here described as social justice is from old-fashioned, without prefix or suffix, justice. On socialist assumptions it may be fairness. But at least on more traditional nonsocialist assumptions it is scarcely justice. (The most famous favorable account of such social justice is provided by Rawls 1971.)

5.25 Much that has been said earlier in this book must by now appear obvious. But obviousness is not something which should always be despised. There are many moments when we need to remember that a truism may be both true and important but nevertheless often superciliously and to disastrous effect ignored. Obviousness, too, really is, as truth and validity most emphatically are not, a matter of how it happens to seem to a particular person or set of persons at some particular time or times. What seems obvious to you may well not seem obvious to me; and what once to him appeared obviously untrue may now appear, even to him, an equally obvious truth.

5.26 For instance, it should be obvious to anyone possessed of the most minimal understanding of the nature of deduction that it must be impossible validly to deduce conclusions more precise than the premises from which they are supposed to follow. Yet very able people do sometimes attempt to do this. Or take the philosophical problem of mind and matter—the problem, that is, of the logical relations or lack of logical relations between talk about thought and consciousness, on the one hand, and talk about nonconscious things and nonconscious stuff, on the other hand. Certainly some very able people have attempted to resolve this by proposing so to redefine the word "experience," which at present carries an essential reference to consciousness, that it would refer only to bodily movements, with no embarrassing reference to consciousness at all. Yet this proposal only begins to look sensible if we mistake it that one and the same word "experience" could carry simultaneously both its present and a new and incompatible sense; and hence that experience, which essentially involves consciousness, could be reduced to mere bodily movements, which do not. (For one lucid and extremely readable venture into this area, see Ryle 1949.)

5.27 It is time to say something more about what can and cannot be achieved by definition. First, it is just worth saying that there is no call to try to define every term. Definition of one word in terms of other words can be profitable only insofar as there are other words that are already sufficiently understood. To demand either a definition or any other kind of explanation where there is no relevant confusion or uncertainty to be removed is tiresome and obstructive. There could be no better authority here than Dr. Samuel Johnson (1709–1784), the compiler of the first substantial and, in its day, comprehensive *Dictionary of the English Language* (1755). According to James Boswell's *Life of Johnson*, he once said: "Sometimes things may be made darker by definition. I see a cow; I define . . . 'Animal quadrupes ruminans cornutum.' But a goat ruminates, and a cow may have no horns. 'Cow' is plainer." I think, too, of a *New Yorker* cartoon that showed an indignant wife confronting her contentedly drunken husband: "No, I will not begin by defining 'soused'!"

5.28 Nor, second, is the ability to produce an adequate definition a necessary condition for possessing a sufficient understanding of the meaning of a term. It is tempting, but wrong, to argue with the Socrates of Plato's *Republic* that: "if I do not know what justice is, I can scarcely know whether it is a virtue or not, and whether its possessor is or is not happy" (354C). For one may be able to employ some word correctly and with understanding on all ordinary occasions without being able to respond to such a "What is . . .?" question with a formal definition.

5.29 It is a point made in his own way by St. Augustine (354–430 C.E.), one of the Four Great Doctors of the Christian Church, in his *Confessions* (400 C.E.): "And I confess to thee, O Lord, that I still do not know what time is, while . . . I know that I am saying this in time" (XI [xxv]). Certainly this venial ignorance did not stop him and will not stop us from employing ordinary temporal expressions correctly and with understanding. We all know perfectly well what he meant when in his unregenerate days he prayed: "O give me chastity, but not just yet!"

5.30 The moral is that we need definition or other explication only where there already is, or where we may reasonably expect that there will be, some relevant confusion or uncertainty about meaning. A third point is that in such suitable cases for treatment the right prescription is not always a formal definition beginning "X is . . ." or, better, "The word x means. . . ." Suppose someone is talking about alienation. If that person gives us a definition, this will most likely be in terms of other theoretical notions derived from the young Karl Marx. But what is really required is some indication of how this theory engages with, and of how its truth value might be determined by reference to, what actually happens. Hence, the illuminating question is not: "How would you define the word 'alienation'?" but "How could you tell that a person was or was not or was no longer alienated?" When, but only when, we are equipped with workable criteria for alienation can we entertain such theories as possible contributions to sociology as a science (see paragraphs 3.17–3.22).

5.31 A fourth point, already suggested in the previous three paragraphs, is that definitions are of words or their meanings and not of whatever the words might be used to refer to. It is good practice always to bring this out by putting both the word or expression to be defined (Latin, the *definiendum*) and the supposed or proposed equivalent (correspondingly, the *definiens*) between quotation marks. The act of definition thus consists in saying either that the *definiendum* is or that it is to be equivalent in meaning to the *definiens*. Where the claim is that by established correct usage the two already are equivalent, we speak of a descriptive definition. Where some innovation is involved, we speak of a prescriptive or stipulative definition.

5.32 Some people who grasp our fourth point too well may, like Humpty Dumpty, be carried away by the possibilities of stipulative redefinition. Remember that often-quoted exchange from chapter 6 of Lewis Carroll's *Through the Looking Glass*:

> "I don't know what you mean by 'glory,'" Alice said. Humpty Dumpty smiled contemptuously. "Of course you don't—till I tell you. I meant 'there's a nice knock-down argument for you!'" "But 'glory' doesn't mean 'a knock-down argument,'" Alice objected. "When I use a word," Humpty Dumpty said in rather a scornful tone, "it means just what I choose it to mean—neither more nor less." "The question is," said Alice, "whether you can make words mean so many different things." "The question is," said Humpty Dumpty, "Which is to be master—that's all."

5.33 Certainly it is a matter of human choice rather than natural law that in particular languages particular sounds and particular collections of letters have the meanings they have. Yet this fact of ultimate and collective human decision must not be mistaken to imply that it is either right or possible for any of us individually to endow any such shape or sound with whatever meaning we may happen to wish on it.

5.34 It was all very well for whoever first introduced the concept of gas to give its present employment to the previously unemployed monosyllable "gas." It is a different thing altogether to announce that you now propose to use some already serving word in a sense other than that determined by what is now established usage. Again I quote Dr. Johnson, although he brings in the rather special case of names: "My name might have been 'Nicholson' originally as well as 'Johnson'; but if you were to call me Nicholson now, you would call me very absurdly."

5.35 To do what Humpty Dumpty did and what too many real people also do is not merely to speak "very absurdly." It is also to act in bad faith. For to express oneself in a public language is to undertake to speak and ask to be understood in accordance with the established meaning conventions of that language. So to say something in some public language and then afterward to insist that you intended it to be interpreted in accordance with some private and previously unexplained personal conventions of your own is to break the contract which you implicitly made when you started to speak in that language.

5.36 The fact that it is dishonest to make substantial departures from accepted usage without due notice is, however, no reason to rule out all stipulative redefinition. Like all other human institutions languages can be made better, as well as worse, by deliberate acts of policy. But reformers do need to take full account of the facts that linguistic habits are habits and that, like other habits, they take a lot of changing (see paragraph 4.12). It is one thing to stipulate a meaning for a fresh term. This is to ask us to acquire the corresponding fresh verbal habits. It is quite another to prescribe a change in the meaning of a familiar word. This is to demand not only that we learn new skills and new associations but also that we unlearn old ones. This unlearning can be difficult and slow. Some people may never achieve it, even if they do really try to do so.

5.37 If, therefore, we want to advance understanding and to communicate in a straightforward way, we shall not propose new senses going clear against the grain of current usage. Any redefinitions of familiar everyday words will involve modest redirections, not revolutionary reversals. One classic object lesson in what not to do is provided by the American sociologist Thorstein Veblen (1857–1929). In *The Theory of the Leisure Class* (1899) he introduces the expression "conspicuous waste" in a technical sense, stipulating most emphatically that in his book it is not to carry the customary overtones of condemnation. As he ought to have realized, and perhaps did, such old and strong associations cannot and will not be broken at a stroke. It soon becomes clear that he himself, like his readers, continues to construe "conspicuous waste" in an unfavorable sense (Veblen 1899, pp. 97ff.). What pretends to be neutral and impartial social science thus becomes partisan sociological moralizing.

5.38 Mention of Veblen's characteristic employment of the expression "conspicuous waste" leads us to notice that many words and phrases carry such built-in value commitments. Since Aristotle first made this observation in his *Nicomachean Ethics* (1107A9–12), literary critics, psychologists, linguists, philosophers, and others have given a deal of attention to this fact and have developed various distinctions: between neutral or purely descriptive meaning on the one hand, and expressive, emotive, normative, or evaluational on the other. In a short introductory book such as this one I cannot afford to say very much about these distinctions. But there are three points that absolutely must be made.

5.39 The first is that there is nothing wrong with the second sort of meanings nor with the words whose meanings are partly or wholly of this second sort, as such. If there were it would paradoxically be wrong to say so. For the word "wrong" is obviously one that must itself fall under any such all-inclusive embargo. (Compare the rebuke once allegedly characteristic of "progressive" parenting: "You mustn't say anything is wrong. That is very naughty.")

5.40 Of course, excessive employment of incendiary terms will prevent or disrupt rational discussion of the issues so presented. Heat is frequently the enemy of light. But to prohibit all purely or partly evaluative language is to put every form of valuation beyond the pale of rationality. The now popular misconception that this is how things are or ought to be does a lot to bring about a state in which, in the words of the Irish poet W. B. Yeats:

> The best lack all conviction, while the worst
> Are full of passionate intensity.
>   ("Second Coming")

5.41 The truth is that it is neither relevant nor sensible to object that discourse contains emotive words and value judgments, if its object just was to establish conclusions about what attitudes ought to be adopted or what action ought to be taken. What is offensive to reason and what does constitute a ground for objection is any arbitrariness in the application of these words or any failure to deploy appropriate good reasons for whatever such judgments are in fact made. Veblen's proceedings were not obnoxious because he was denouncing conspicuous waste. Waste, whether conspicuous or not, ought to be denounced and, even better, stopped. What was wrong was that Veblen was actually denouncing conspicuous waste and wasters while pretending to be a neutral scientist. The point was not that there should not be sociological moralists, but that no one has any business, when acting in that quite different capacity, to wear a scientist's laboratory coat.

5.42 The second point about this second sort of meaning concerns arbitrariness. Everyone can conjugate the highly irregular verb which is supposed to run: "I am firm," "You are obstinate," and "He is pigheaded." It is then easy, and consequently common, to draw the diametrically wrong moral. The temptation is to construe this wayward conjugation as supporting a general theory put forward by the always bold, not to say reckless, Thomas Hobbes. In 1651 he suggested in chapter 6 of *Leviathan* that all terms that carry any meaning of this second sort are to be defined with reference to the speaker: "whatsoever is the object of any man's appetite or desire, that is it which he for his part calleth 'Good'; and the object of his hate and aversion 'Evil,' and of his contempt 'Vile' and 'Inconsiderable.' For these words 'Good,' 'Evil' and 'Contemptible' are ever used with relation to the person that useth them. . . ."

5.43 This Hobbist view is nowadays widely expressed. Although it is popularly known as relativism, it would be better described as subjectivism. It has a strong appeal both to the cynic in all of us and to the secular conviction that value is not a natural fact independent of the existence and activity of the human race, but is somehow a projection of human inclinations and human aversions. But cynicism is not always what it always claims to be: realism. And we have already seen in the surely similar case of meaning that to say that something is not a natural fact independent of all human desire and human choice is not immediately to license the conclusion that it is a creature of any and every individual caprice (see paragraphs 5.32–5.35).

5.44 The crucial objection to this first Hobbist theory was put exactly a century later by David Hume (1711–1776) in his *Inquiry concerning the Principles of Morals* (1748). (Since Hobbes also offered another more social theory, according to which value must be the creature of sovereign power, we could call the present suggestion his Humpty Dumpty thesis.) No one could have been more convinced than

Hume of the fundamental secular point that value is not a natural fact independent of all human beings. Yet he insisted on a distinction: "When a man denominates another his 'enemy,' his 'rival,' his 'antagonist,' his 'adversary,' he is understood to speak the language of self-love, and to express sentiments, peculiar to himself, and arising from his particular circumstances and situation. But when he bestows on any man the epithets of 'vicious' or 'odious' or 'depraved,' he then speaks another language, and expresses sentiments in which he expects all his audience are to concur with him" (IX[i]).

5.45 Because Hobbes and Hume express themselves in the idiom and the prose rhythms of their different centuries both passages may require, as they will certainly reward, a second reading. The upshot is that it must be wrong to abuse words and phrases from Hume's second class by treating them as if they belonged to his first class—the class to which Hobbes apparently wanted to consign all valuing words. Suppose we allow, as we surely must, that all the phases of the supposed irregular verb "I am firm" belong in Hume's second category. Then the man who commends his own conduct as firm, when he would condemn the same conduct in a third person as pig-headed, is being arbitrary. His arbitrariness consists in discriminating between two relevant cases for no good reason. He is like the woman who indignantly denied the charge of hoarding on the grounds that she was only taking care to stock up before the hoarders got everything.

5.46 The conclusion to draw is, therefore, not Hobbist but Humean. Sincere debate about values, and in particular about morals, largely consists in the discovery and removal of such arbitrary discriminations. Furthermore, it is an important part of what it means to maintain that some protest or stand or attitude is moral—as opposed to merely personal or partisan—that that protest or stand or attitude appeals to principles and that the principles to which it appeals are to be applied consistently and impartially, if not universally. Everyone knows why we impugn the sincerity of selective moralists or, better, "moralists." They profess a moral objection to, say, the use of poison gas. But when poison gas is being used by some party they happen to favor then, as the Greek tragedians used to say, a great ox sits on their tongues.

5.47 The third thing to notice in connection with the second sort of meaning is the phenomenon of Persuasive Definition. The phenomenon was first discussed extensively, and this label introduced, by the philosopher C. L. Stevenson. He distinguished between descriptive and emotive meaning using "emotive" in an extremely comprehensive, ragbag sense. Persuasive Definition consists in the attempt to annex either the favorable or the unfavorable emotive meaning of a word to some different descriptive meaning. Adolf Hitler was engaged in persuasive definition when on behalf of his National Socialist German Workers' Party he proclaimed: "National Socialism is true democracy." So were those supposedly at the opposite end of the political spectrum, who christened the Soviet zone of Germany "The German Democratic Republic" and argued for their description (see paragraphs 1.30 and 4.9).

5.48 Perhaps the best explanation and illustration is a passage C. L. Stevenson quotes from Aldous Huxley's *Eyeless in Gaza* (1936):

> "But if you want to be free, you've got to be a prisoner. It's a condition of freedom—true freedom." "True freedom!" Anthony repeated in the parody of a clerical voice. "I always love that kind of argument. The contrary of a thing isn't its contrary; oh dear me no! It's the thing itself but as it *truly* is. Ask any diehard what conservatism is; he'll tell you it's *true* socialism. And the brewer's trade papers: they're full of articles about the beauty of true temperance. Ordinary temperance is just gross refusal to drink; but true temperance, *true* temperance is something much more refined. True temperance is a bottle of claret with each meal and three double whiskies after dinner. . . . What's in a name?" Anthony went on. "The answer is, practically everything, if the name's a good one. Freedom is a marvellous name. That's why you're so anxious to make use of it. You think that if you call imprisonment true freedom, people will be attracted to the prison. And the worst of it is you're quite right." (Quoted in Stevenson 1945, pp. 214–15)

6

Figuring

6.1 The older and wiser geisha of traditional Japan are said to have lived by the maxim: "Where figures are deficient, grace and charm must come to the rescue." But where figures, in another sense, are more abundant neither grace nor charm can substitute for critical alertness. Consider, for instance, the statement that 70 percent of the people currently serving sentences in the prisons of Ruritania have served one or more previous terms. Does this mean that Ruritania is afflicted with a recidivism rate of 70 percent; that is, that 70 percent of those sentenced for the first time come back for more? And if so, are we further entitled to infer that, at least in Ruritania, the threat of prison is as a deterrent largely ineffective?

6.2 A moment's thought will show that the correct answer to both questions is "No." Consider the second question first. Suppose that 70 percent of those sentenced for the first time do come back for more and let us assume also—perhaps too optimistically—that Ruritania's courts never convict the innocent. Then we certainly may, indeed we must, conclude that most of those sentenced for the first time (70 percent, to be precise) are not deterred from committing a second offense. This is a sad, bad business: a series of prison terms is no way to fill a lifetime.

But nothing has been said to preclude the possibility that the existing Ruritanian penal arrangements, whatever their faults, are successfully deterring many others who do not offend but, but for the existence of these arrangements, would offend. The mistake is to overlook that the Ruritanian prison population, precisely because it contains all and only those serving terms of imprisonment, is not a fair sample of the whole adult population of Ruritania.

6.3 Now consider the first proposed conclusion. Given that 70 percent of those currently serving sentences have been in prison before, can we conclude that 70 percent of those imprisoned for the first time come back for more? No, we cannot. Our information is inadequate to support any such conclusion. If we want to know what proportion of first-term convicts eventually graduate into second-term convicts, then we shall have to investigate not the term distribution in the present prison population, but the recidivism pattern revealed by past and future prison records.

6.4 Consideration of this item from the fictitious annual returns of the equally fictitious Ruritanian Department of Justice was intended to show how easy it is to go badly wrong in an important matter by misconstruing even one solitary figure. The lesson should be the more salutary since in this imaginary case we cannot attribute our misinterpretations of the data to the deceitful wiles of someone else. For we were not even entertaining the possibility that the single statistic provided might be itself unreliable. Obviously the possibilities of error will increase with any increase in the quantity and complexity of the statistics available; obviously, too, to broach the question of the reliability of the figures offered is to open up a new dimension of difficulty and maybe duplicity. But people do often exaggerate the importance of the intention to hoodwink others as a cause of the misinterpretation of figures which, if properly understood and correctly interpreted, are quite sufficiently accurate. For most of us, as we shall see, are fully capable of drawing incorrect conclusions without either ourselves or anyone else intending that we should do so.

6.5 Certainly a scandalous amount of hocus-pocus with statistics is executed in the frequently fulfilled intention of deceiving other people about what various figures, which are in themselves uncorrupted, do really prove. But there is also an abundance of self-deception, as well as a deal of error which is not the result of bad faith on anyone's part. Since this book is for those who want to improve their own thinking, it is right to concentrate upon our own intellectual lapses and self-deceits. It would no doubt be more agreeable to pillory such notorious public enemies as dishonest advertisers and demagogic politicians. But better thinking, like charity and overpopulation, begins at home. Nor should we forget that demagogues, precisely because they do as such court popularity, would have no incentive to twist and misinterpret the data were there no public eager to applaud shabby maneuvers in support of comfortable prejudices (see paragraph 1.58).

6.6 Another thing that first example was intended to suggest is that there is in our time no escape from figures. The only choice is whether to misinterpret them or whether to interpret them correctly. It is not only that again and again the best evidence is quantitative, although this is both true and important. It is also that many of the most disputed contemporary issues are themselves essentially quantitative. For instance, questions about pollution and about conservation are in practice nearly always questions about how much contamination or how much culling is tolerable. (See paragraph 7.43 for yet another kind of important, essentially quantitative question; namely, that of the poisonness or otherwise of different substances.) For example, we hear that the additional radiation risk consequent upon the commissioning of a new atomic power station in a certain place would be about the same as that already arising from the natural background in that same place. Reassured by the thought that what is natural must be all right—a thought that will have to be subjected to severe critical examination in chapter 7—we fail to notice that this statistic could equally correctly and no less honestly be presented as showing what would surely be felt to be an equally alarming doubling of what had been or would have been the previous risk.

6.7 To appreciate the significance of one statistic, we often need to deploy some others as benchmarks. To know whether we ought to be alarmed or reassured in the present case we shall need to discover what the natural radiation risk was in the area in question and the factor by which a doubling of the radiation index increases the risks. The answers to these questions, too, will have to be specified in figures. Then, to understand how seriously we ought to be worried we shall need to make comparisons, which will be equally quantitative, with other more familiar dangers: those, say, of being a casualty in a road accident or those of birth defects that are not consequences of radiation exposure. No one who is intelligently concerned to produce actual improvements, rather than simply to acquire a reputation for caring, can afford to accept the irrational if perhaps endearing advice once given by the editor of an Anarchist daily newspaper in Spain: "Let us have no more of these miserable statistics, which only freeze the brain and paralyze the blood" (quoted in Brenan 1943, p. 155n.).

6.8 The truth is that it is impossible for human beings or for the members of any other species of living things to live at all without thereby becoming exposed to risks. The reason why people in several of what are certainly the richest, most healthy, and most long-lived human societies which have ever existed appear to be so extraordinarily worried about perceived dangers to their lives and to their health is, surely, that the constant and perhaps exponential growth of human knowledge is necessarily producing ever more knowledge of the innumerable risks to which we may be exposed? Since it is impossible for us either to know all the risks to which we may possibly be exposed or to live without being exposed to any risks at all we have either individually or somehow collectively to make decisions about which risks to identify and to try to diminish or to escape. (For an examination of more and less rational reactions to this inescapable human predicament, see Douglas and Wildavsky 1983).

6.9 Consider again the case of the doubling of the radiation risks in some area by the commissioning in it of a nuclear power station. Our understanding of these particular risks will be transformed totally by the knowledge that almost everything is to some minute degree naturally radioactive and that the risks, if any, from such minute amounts of radioactivity are negligible. Thus, the Nobel laureate Rosalyn Yalow testified to the U.S. Congress that: "As an adult, living human being, my body contains natural radioactivity: 0.1 microcuries of potassium-40 and 0.1 microcuries of carbon-14. According to the current rules of the NRC . . . if I were a laboratory animal who had received this amount of radioactivity as 'by-product material' and died with the radioactivity still in my body, I could not be buried, burned or disposed of in the garbage" (quoted in Efron 1984, p. 409). It was facts of this sort that induced the late Petr Beckmann, author of *The Health Hazards of NOT Going Nuclear* (1976) and founding editor of *Access to Energy*, to issue bumper stickers bearing the legend "Ralph Nader Is Radioactive."

6.10 The first essentials for appreciating the significance or lack of significance of statistics of the sort with which the media confront the general public are in no way technical. What is needed first, and most, and all the time, is an unspecialized critical alertness. This is what we show when we refuse to draw wrong conclusions from the news that 70 percent of the present prison population of Ruritania have already served one or more previous terms or that the commissioning of a nuclear power plant in some area will result in a doubling of the former and natural amount of radiation in that area.

6.11 Another simple, but to many misleading, example is provided by those who cite statistics supposedly showing that the traditional nuclear family is already an anachronism. Only some 26 percent of households, they say, consist of two-parent families and their children. This sounds small. No doubt, too, it is substantially smaller than the percentage would have been a century ago when both the average number of children in each household was larger and the average age of adult death was lower. But what makes this figure of 26 percent so grossly misleading is that it excludes both the households of all who are not yet and perhaps never will be parents and the households of all parents whose children have grown up and left home. To appreciate this requires no familiarity with the notion of statistical significance nor any ability to make Chi-square tests, although it would be desirable to introduce both these things into the compulsory element of everyone's education. What is required is only common sense—sometimes, it would seem, a somewhat scarce commodity.

6.12 Another simple but more important example is the figures supposedly showing that women earn less than men. The actual figures reported, of course, vary from year to year and from country to country. But all those which I have myself come across during the last twenty years have indicated that the earnings of women were between only 59 percent and only 75 percent of the earnings of men. Always these figures have been presented as revealing a situation considered to be self-evidently scandalous. If these percentages were percentages of what men were being paid for the same numbers of hours of the same kinds of work, then the situations in the countries concerned would indeed be self-evidently scandalous. But in countries of the kind in which such statistics are regularly compiled, published, and widely discussed it is by now probably illegal and in any case practically impossible for employers to pay women less for the same number of hours of the same sort of work.

6.13 Of course, even where there are such laws it is likely that there will be at least some evasion and some breaches of these laws, and much more evasion and more breaches in some countries than in others. But by far the greater part of the explanation of such substantial percentage differences must surely lie in the effects on women of childbearing and child raising. These activities result in women averaging fewer hours of work in the year (as part-timers) and fewer years on a given job than men. Add to these causes the facts that there are physically demanding and well-paid fields which women seldom enter—mining, lumberjacking, and construction work, for example. There are also other less physically demanding well-paid fields in which a strong mathematics background is required—something which is even rarer among women than among men. Even with all of this it seems that, at least in the United States, the really big difference in income is not between men and women but between married women and everyone else. (See, for instance, Sowell 1984, chapter 5.)

6.14 You may want to remove some or all of these and various other differences—of these and various other inequalities—between men and women. But you will, I hope, not want to claim that the inequalities in earnings which are the results of marriage and motherhood are as self-evidently unfair and scandalous as they certainly would be were they the results of employers paying women less for the same number of hours of the same kinds of work than they were paying men. If it is for any reason thought desirable to reduce these particular inequalities, then this reduction will presumably have to be achieved by the provision of substantial state subsidies for mothers who are caring for their own children and/or by the maintenance of a National Child Care Service. Such policies would obviously have substantial tax implications, which is neither to assert nor to imply anything about their acceptability.

6.15 Finally, it is also worth noting two other important inequalities between the life situations of men and women, inequalities rarely mentioned in this kind of context. For the last several decades the suicide rate among American men has been more than three times that among American women, whereas in all First World countries we find that however much the life expectancy for men rises, it never catches up to equal that for women. One shudders to think of the policies which might be formulated to remove or reduce these two inequalities! (Levin 1987 and Goldberg 1993 can be strongly recommended to feminists eager to face and to attempt to overcome a powerful intellectual challenge.)

6.16 These days the sorts of inequalities most regularly discussed and researched are those of income and wealth. These discussions and also the researches to which they refer are often vitiated by distorting malpractices. For instance, it will not do, notwithstanding that it is done daily, to compare one person's weekly wage with another person's annual salary. To do this is to cheat. It is to misrepresent one of the two terms in the chosen comparison by a factor of fifty-two.

6.17 Again it will not do, notwithstanding that this too is done daily, to compare one person's take-home pay after tax and all other stoppages and subtractions with someone else's gross income. This malpractice is especially deceitful in countries with more or less fiercely progressive taxation on incomes. For it is a defining characteristic of any system of progressive taxation—as opposed to proportionate taxation or to poll taxation—that it should diminish the real differences, net of tax, between any extremes of gross income. To leave the impact of progressive taxation out of account must be, therefore, to exaggerate the differences in spendable income net of tax. The cheat is compounded when, as here, the effect of taxation is neglected in only one of the two terms of the comparison.

6.18 These are strong words condemning flagrant misdemeanors. Such condemnation is likely to stir up a storm of defenders: "What do you expect a labor union leader to say?" Well, we ought all to expect (prescriptive) labor union leaders, and everyone else, to present an honest case honestly argued; although I am afraid experience has taught us that this is not always to be expected (descriptive) either of labor union leaders or of many other people—sometimes including, perhaps, even ourselves (see paragraphs 5.14 and 5.19).

6.19 Those same defenders may state: "But you can understand why people think up these twisted comparisons and cherish them." Certainly, we all can. But the point was precisely and only to bring out that and how they are twisted, and thereby to make such malpractices fractionally less frequent and less welcome. We all know too why people cheat on their tax returns. But that is not in itself an objection to the endeavors of the United States Internal Revenue Service (IRS) to make such cheating less common. We have here a fresh species within the genus Subject/Motive Shift (see paragraphs 4.3, 4.13–4.14, and 4.17–4.18). Let it be simultaneously both christened and pilloried the But-you-can-understand-why Evasion.

6.20 One possible and very salutary response to misrepresentations, and one which is appropriate to them all and not only to those of the kinds so far considered, is to point out that, in general, unsound argument and outright misrepresentation should tend to discredit the causes which they are recruited to serve. If spokespersons have to multiply the actual difference by fifty-two in order to seem to justify their indignation, then the uncommitted critic should surely be inclined to conclude that the present position is nothing like so obnoxious as these spokespersons have been trying to make out. If controversialists deliberately misrepresent the positions of their opponents or knowingly employ fallacious arguments against them, then those opponents are fully entitled, and would be well advised, to insist that this misbehavior constitutes a tacit and reluctant admission that their own actual position is one which the misbehaver is altogether unable validly to refute.

6.21 Statistics about poverty can also be misleading without anyone having been or being deliberately and, so to speak, straightforwardly dishonest in either their compilation or their employment. For a start there is the possible and often-realized confusion about the actual composition of the set of the poorest 10 percent, whether it is individuals or households which are being counted. We must never assume, because it is never true, that the membership of either set in one year will be exactly the same even in the immediately following year. But both the nature and the extent of the membership changes will differ from time to time and from place to place. Only if a large proportion of the members are found to remain members for many years will there be any reason to speak of a class of the poor.

6.22 But before we can sensibly discuss whether there is or is not a class of the poor we must have a working definition of "poverty." All accepted definitions are no doubt to some extent relative to the actual condition of the better-off in the society in question. But this modest relativity must be sharply distinguished from that of the definitions of those who identify poverty more or less completely with inequality and consequently define the poor as those each enjoying an income of less than such and such a percentage of whatever is the local average income.

6.23 The introduction of such definitions is one way to discover more poverty for welfare states to combat. Another is simply to ignore some people's actual sources of income in cash and/or in kind. In the United States, for instance, official statisticians have enormously exaggerated the actual extent of deprivation by counting only cash incomes and ignoring Aid to Families with Dependent Children (AFDC), food stamps, subsidized housing, free medical care, and other forms of tax-financed and state-supplied income in kind. Indeed the official census data are based on samples in which subjects are not even asked whether they receive food stamps, live in public housing, or are eligible for Medicaid. Furthermore, if we are genuinely concerned to discover the actual standard of living enjoyed or suffered by the clients of a welfare state we need to inquire without prejudice how many of those clients contrive to acquire incomes in cash and in kind larger than those they receive in a variety of tax-funded handouts. Such investigations have been made in the United Kingdom, and have revealed that the actual incomes are on average significantly larger. In part these additions represent casual earnings in the black economy, in part gifts from friends and relations, and in part what can only be described as miscellaneous. (Here I am reminded of a *New Yorker* cartoon in which a taxpayer is shown expostulating to an IRS official. The caption read: "What do you mean 'clarify miscellaneous'? What do you think that word is for?")

6.24 Consider, to go back a bit, yet another kind of unfair financial comparison. Suppose that a large sum of money is mentioned. Before responding we should take care to ask ourselves to what in the present context it is relevant to relate this sum? If we are to respond sensibly we must have benchmarks to guide us. We have perhaps seen a headline screaming that some company has accumulated profits running into hundreds of millions of dollars. Before remarking sourly and suspiciously that that is where the money goes, we should ask what these millions amount to as a percentage return on capital employed or how they compare with the company's wage bill or with its total sales. These are the comparisons which are relevant if we are thinking of the profits as booty available for a shareout among either the company's shareholders or its employees or its customers, or—of course—the IRS. Nor should we ever forget that in such cases the IRS always gets two cuts, one directly out of the company's profits and then another out of the shareholders' income from shares in that company. And, if the subject of our discussion were the U.S. federal budget, we should have to recall that famously wry remark of Senator Everett Dirksen: "A billion here and a billion there, and soon you are beginning to talk of real money."

6.25 When we ask the right questions about figures and actually do relevant rough calculations, we may be surprised by what we find. We certainly shall be when we turn from questions about income to questions about wealth. The distinction is important. It is as easy as it is common to think of all wealth as available for spending. If any individual comes into a bit of money from a legacy or wins a cash prize in a lottery or is given some special bonus, then there is little to stop the spending of the whole lot in one gigantic spree. But it is a very different story if we are talking about the wealth of a nation. Most of this is in the form either of the physical means of production or of the residences of the population and the miscellaneous equipment of its daily living. We cannot collectively sell off any of these assets and spend the proceeds without thereby prejudicing our collective prospects of earning and enjoying a tolerable living in the future.

6.26 We have here another instance of a general truth exemplified differently in chapter 5 (see especially paragraphs 5.22–5.23). We are not entitled to assume either that what applies to the whole of some group taken collectively applies equally to any and every individual member of that group or the other way around. Consider another example: Anyone can park here at any time, but it does not follow that everyone can do so simultaneously or even successively. The crucial practical difference is that while not everyone wants to park here, or at any rate not at the same times, almost everyone would like to lay their hands on some of someone else's wealth and to spend it as their own income.

6.27 In many countries, though perhaps less frequently in the United States than elsewhere, people are forever coming up with figures supposedly showing that some percent of all the wealth in that country is owned by a relatively tiny proportion of the total population. Before entering into any discussion of what, if anything, needs to be done about this alleged fact we need first to ask both where these figures come from and upon what principles they were compiled. Unless we have some satisfactory answer to the first of these two preliminary questions, we have no guarantee that the figures were not simply invented.

6.28 Of course here and now and in this matter it is unlikely that such figures would be invented. But it is well to remember that both the U.S. Central Intelligence Agency (CIA) and some leading U.S. economists were apparently misled by their study of official Soviet statistics to believe, until nearly the time when its collapse became notorious, that the Soviet economy was healthy. We may also recall the story of the very senior judge in the former British Indian Empire who told a young (British) civil servant: "When you are a bit older you will not quote Indian statistics with that assurance . . . what you must never forget is that every one of those comes in the first instance from the *chowty dar* [village watchman], who just puts down what he damn well pleases."

6.29 It is important to press the second question too. Users of statistics, unlike users of television sets, need to know something about how the constituent materials were originally gathered and later cobbled together. Without this information we may easily draw unwarranted conclusions. If the figures referred to the United Kingdom, for instance, we should need to ask whether they were compiled from the Inheritance Tax returns and, if so, what if any allowance was made for the fact that most estates are too small to attract this tax? The sum of all these individually small estates could very well be, relative to the sum of all the biggest estates, large. Whether or not it in fact is, is the main part of precisely the point which is here in question.

6.30 Again, what allowance, if any, was made for pension rights and life insurance policies? The former escape the Inheritance Tax net completely, whereas the latter, insofar as they are caught, are bound to come up tagged with a higher value than any that could have been imputed earlier. Yet pension rights and life insurance policies, usually backed by investments held in the name of some corporation, must during life constitute a significant proportion of the wealth, such as it may be, of most middle-class people.

6.31 The *Economist*, a journal published in London but having much larger circulation outside the United Kingdom than in it, in 1973 made and published some calculations about the distribution of wealth in an imaginary country, not Ruritania this time but Egalitaria. These calculations are relevant to us in three ways. First, they constitute another and even more impressive example showing how unexpected may be the results revealed by still not intolerably difficult calculations. Second, they underline the curiously neglected importance of the fact that people progress through life cycles from infancy to old age. We can scarcely expect, in either sense of "expect" (see paragraphs 5.14, 5.19, and 6.18), to be in the same financial situation at every stage in our particular life cycle. This is one of the reasons why the membership of the set of the poorest 10 percent in one country in one year will not be exactly the same as its membership in the following year and in the year after that. Third, they spell out some of the unnoticed implications of one set of egalitarian ideals. They thus provide those who nourish such ideals with a very necessary frame of reference, enabling them to assess more accurately how far and where the actual situation falls short of their own aspirations.

6.32 According to the *Economist*, all Egalitarians are educated in public schools up to the age of twenty-one, with no opportunity at this stage to earn enough to save. All men then work for the same wage till sixty-five, when they retire on full pay. Women work for only twenty nonchildbearing years but in those years get equal pay, with the same pension rights, as men. Inheritance is forbidden, but all earners and all pensioners save exactly 10 percent of their incomes, investing their savings in state bonds yielding 10 percent compound interest. This high rate perhaps compensates for the absolute embargo on all capital appreciation. The roundness of the figure also simplifies the arithmetic, as do two further stipulations: the net reproduction rate has been unity for the past eighty-five years and everyone dies on their eighty-fifth birthday. So how much of the privately owned wealth in Egalitaria is owned by the richest 10 percent of the whole population? "The answer seems to be that the wealthiest 10 percent of Egalitarians (who by definition are all the men aged from sixty-eight to eighty-four inclusive) must now own about 74 percent of the privately owned wealth . . ." (May 26, 1973, pp. 16–18).

6.33 In many, perhaps all, countries the tale is told of a stranger asking a villager for directions and receiving the response: "If I wanted to go there, I would not start from here." The question of the baseline from which they start is often crucial for appreciating the actual implications of a set of statistics. A once well-known study of crime in the United States set out to refute the notion that Supreme Court decisions of the Earl Warren era caused the subsequent soaring rise in the rates of crime. Charles Silberman argued that at the time of his writing, the courts "prosecute, convict and incarcerate a larger proportion of those arrested for a felony today than did *courts of the 1920s*" (Silberman 1978, p. 261, emphasis added). But the era of the Warren Court began not in the 1920s or even in the 1930s but in 1953, and its landmark criminal law decisions are largely from the 1960s—*Mapp* v. *Ohio* (1961), *Gideon* v. *Wainwright* (1963), *Escobedo* v. *Illinois* (1964), and *Miranda* v. *Arizona* (1966). Crime statistics based on the actual chronology of the Warren Court show that if the thesis Silberman was so eager to refute is to be refuted at all, then the materials for that refutation will have to be found somewhere else, as, in a way, Silberman himself seems to have appreciated.

6.34 When Earl Warren became chief justice in 1953, the homicide rate in the United States was 4.8 for every one hundred thousand of the population—lower than it had been for four decades. The total number

of criminal homicides in American urban centers of twenty-five thousand or more people was no higher in 1953 than it had been in 1937,
even though the population of such urban centers had grown by more
than 19 percent between 1940 and 1950 alone. In short, the Warren
Court inherited not only a low homicide rate but one of which the overall
trend was not rising. Yet a sharp rise in homicide began in the 1960s.
The rate more than doubled from 1963 to 1971. (See, for instance,
Sowell 1986a, chapter 9; cf. Wilson 1975.)

6.35 A more recent and indisputably decisive example of misleading by the choice of a particular baseline is provided by the report
of the generously financed and staffed Joseph Rowntree Foundation,
Inquiry into Income and Wealth (Hills et al. 1995). These researchers
started by so defining "poverty" that in any country a household must be
accounted poor if it receives less than half of whatever are the average
earnings in that country—a definition which, they assure us, is generally accepted and employed by social scientists. Using that definition
they were able to find that between 1979 and 1992—note these dates—
the proportion of the U.K. population to be accounted poor had risen
from 7 to 25 percent. The publication of their report was rewarded by
banner headlines. For lay persons, unaware of the social scientific definition of "poverty," were bound to misunderstand it as having claimed
to have discovered, in a country which is by world standards unusually
prosperous, no less than fourteen million people whom such lay persons
would account to be poor. But our concern here is with the second main
finding in this report. That was that the formidable increases in van-
dalism, burglary, and violent crime that occurred between 1979 and
1992 are to be attributed to parallel increases during the same period in
unemployment, in inequality (the gap between the highest and the
lowest incomes), and in poverty, as we are told that poverty is defined by
social scientists.

6.36 The stated reason for adopting 1979 as the baseline was that
1979 was the year in which the first of a new series of official British
Crime Surveys was published. It is obvious that for these researchers a
further reason was that 1979 was the year in which, as a result of a general election, the Conservative party led by Margaret Thatcher entered
office. The researchers, of course, had every right to abhor Thatcher, her

administrations, and all their works. But as professed social scientists they ought to have been especially thorough and conscientious in their testing of a hypothesis which they so very strongly wanted to believe was true. Instead they revealed a breathtaking indifference to what surely were undisputed and decisively falsifying facts.

6.37 For example, their own report shows that the period 1961–1979 was one of rising incomes, declining absolute and relative poverty, and, for most of the time, uniquely low unemployment. It was also a period of rapidly rising recorded crime, riot, and drug abuse. Yet these researchers do not attempt to explain how and why these facts consist with their hypothesis. Nor do they attempt to test that hypothesis by reference to earlier periods during which there was far more unemployment, more absolute poverty, and more inequality between the best off and the worst off than between 1979 and 1992 and during which there was also far less crime than at any time between 1961 and 1992. (For an exhaustive critique of this disgraceful report, see Dennis 1997.)

6.38 Where there clearly is some historical trend, before-and-after studies can be especially misleading—even to those less eager to be misled! Suppose, for instance, that in some country there has been a long-term decline in the annual total of fatal automobile accidents. Then, if some piece of automobile safety legislation is introduced, it will be difficult or impossible to determine what part if any of any subsequent decline in the accident rate was produced by that legislation. Understandably, the backers of the legislation will claim that the decline was all their own work. But how, if at all, can they show that they are not committing the Whatever-follows-must-be-the-consequence Fallacy (see paragraph 1.53) and that the decline would not have occurred even without the legislation?

6.39 A main theme of the present chapter is that what is needed first, most, and all the time is not technical expertise in statistics or anything else, but an unspecialized critical alertness. The way to acquire this or any other disposition is by practice. To make clear that it is a lay rather than an expert business it may help if some of the practice is on specialists, and these specialists on what they see as their best behavior as specialists. For example, many years ago Edmund Leach, who was in his day one of the leading British anthropologists, was invited by the

British Broadcasting Corporation (BBC) to deliver the lectures in a prestigious annual series. These lectures were afterward printed in the BBC's weekly journal *The Listener*. In one of them Leach asserted, very confidently, that although "Admittedly the statistics show a numerical increase in the incidence of crime . . . this is a measure of police efficiency, not of the moral state of the nation. Crimes are created by Parliament: it needs a policeman to make a criminal" (November 30, 1967).

6.40 Certainly it is true, true by definition, that in the legal sense of the term "crime," what is and is not here and now a crime is determined by what the law says. Private homosexual relations between consenting men over twenty-one years old ceased to be criminal in England on the day when the corresponding change in the law took effect. So there is a sense in which British criminals are made (not by British policemen and policewomen but) by the British Parliament. But from this definitional premise we are not entitled to deduce the massively substantial conclusion that either the British legal system is or the British policepersons are in fact so counterproductive as actually to induce people to perform actions of the kinds proscribed as criminal. The point simply is that the British Parliament determines what kinds of actions are to be proscribed as criminal, not that it makes people perform such actions. Leach was misled into uttering this piece of nonsense by his desire to ally himself with numerous social-scientific colleagues who were at that time attempting to persuade the lay public that what we believed to be (and now know to have been) a rising tide of crime was in truth the merely imaginary product of a "moral panic."

6.41 This is one more occasion where we need the fundamental distinction between propositions that are analytic and logically necessary, and propositions that are synthetic and contingent (see paragraphs 3.4–3.17 and 3.29–3.30). A similar fallacious move is sometimes made in Third World First circles. For it is necessarily true that the rich make the poor and the other way around but only in the factitious sense that such correlative terms as "rich" and "poor" depend for their meaning upon the possibility of mutual contrast. From this alone we cannot legitimately infer—what I am not here either asserting or denying—that rich men and rich countries always and everywhere somehow grind the faces and pick the pockets of the poor.

6.42 Having explained the nature of the mistake Leach made, we can now go on to ask how he was misled into making it. It can be seen as a case of sophistication going to the head. The sophistication is to be aware, in general, that even the most honestly and competently compiled figures may not mean what they seem to mean, and, in particular, that they may sometimes tell us more about the method of compilation than about their supposed subject. Yet to assume that this must always be so, or to assume without particular reason that it is so in some particular case, is to be infatuated with one's own insight. However, there but for the grace of God go we. For when we first become acquainted with some fallacy, as students of the present book need to recognize, it can be almost irresistibly tempting to identify arguments as tokens of this fallacy type when what we really have is either a token of some other type or even no fallacy at all (see paragraphs 1.49–1.54).

6.43 The insight by which Leach allowed himself to be carried away is important, and it provides one of the reasons why we have to ask both where figures come from and upon what principles they were compiled. All U.K. crime statistics at the time when Leach was lecturing were compiled by the police, who were required to include all but only crimes reported to police officers. Since that was also the time when sexual relations between consenting (or active!) adult men had only very recently been decriminalized, students of the criminal statistics were all very much aware that the rise in the number of successful prosecutions recorded in some particular area might previously have indicated not a rise in the number of such offenses committed, but the recent appointment of a notorious homophobe as chief constable for that area.

6.44 Indeed my own favorite headline from that earlier period— "Wave of Buggery in Bootle"—may actually have pointed not to a rise but to a decline in the number of offenses committed. For some potential offenders may have been deterred by news of the successful prosecutions and punishment of offenders. In that case the headline ought to have been "New Broom Sweeps Bootle's Buggers," giving discredit where discredit was due.

6.45 Legend also tells, I know not whether truly or falsely, of an eager woman who as a research student carried out a wide and weary psychometric program, coming up eventually with the agreeable finding that the average IQ of men is equal to the average IQ of women. It must have been hard to tell her that one of the specifications for the particular battery of tests she was applying was that the tests chosen to constitute her battery must yield this result. Whether this sexist legend is true or false we do still need to recognize that sometimes batteries of tests and other systems of inquiry may be deliberately designed and required to produce some of the particular findings which they do produce.

6.46 Today the most familiar examples are those test batteries that are designed and required to ensure that different subsets in the populations taking these tests, whether those subsets are racially or ethnically or however else defined, are represented in the outcomes in proportion to their representation in the total populations of which they are subsets. The one thing that needs to be said about these proceedings is that it is viciously circular to maintain, as all too often is maintained, that some particular test battery is biased if you can offer no other or better reason for so insisting than that it fails to produce some desired and no doubt politically correct result.

6.47 That Karl Pearson (1857–1936), a leading statistician and philosopher of science, once published a paper entitled "The Scientific Aspect of Monte Carlo Roulette" is not legend but history. With appropriate qualifications, his conclusion was that "roulette as played at Monte Carlo is not a game of chance." This result was derived from his analysis of the outcomes of every spin made, day by day and week by week, for many months. These outcomes were all recorded, for the benefit of seekers for systems, in a paper called *Le Monaco*. It later emerged that the reporter assigned to this dispiriting task had preferred to sit out his days at a nearby café rather than to stand on tiptoe peering at the tables in the casino. So Pearson's statistical analysis was really not evidence of some hidden and perhaps exploitable physical regularities in those spinning wheels, but evidence for the more general psychological fact that if we try to think up, straight out of our own heads, a genuinely random series, we shall not succeed.

6.48 One mistake in the interpretation of statistics often made by otherwise wide-awake students of social affairs and disputants about social policy is to argue that, because the distribution of some characteristic among persons who are all at one extreme in respect of that characteristic may not account for much of any differences among their achievements, therefore that characteristic may be altogether unimportant for the securing of such achievements. Since top basketball players who are six-foot-ten are not noticeably better than those who are only six-foot-nine, an argument on these lines would leave unexplained the fact that in this field the professionals all tower over the rest of us. Again, "At a college where virtually all students score in the top 10 percent on national tests, just where in that select group a particular student is located probably means much less than . . . motivation, emotional state, and other such personal factors. . . . But to use this as a reason to admit students from the *bottom* half of the test scores to compete with those at the top is to set the stage for disaster. The 1960s saw this kind of reasoning, and these kinds of disasters, on college campuses across the country" (Sowell 1984, p. 129, emphasis original).

6.49 Certainly it is vital to be alert to the possibility that figures may simply have been conjured out of the air. We need always to be ready with the equivalent of the question asked of strangers in old-time Westerns: "Where you from?" Always, too, we need to be aware of the possibility that what the statistics in front of us now do really reveal is, if anything, something about the conditions of their compilation rather than something about what they seem or purport to record. But these are only occasionally realized possibilities. They are not general necessities. No recognition of the dangers of mendacity, ingenuous error, and self-deceit ought to blind us to the indispensable necessity in so many fields of quantitative evidence and quantitative thinking (see paragraph 6.6). If we are committed to the improvement of our understandings we must categorically reject as obscurantist the pseudosophisticated slogan: "There are lies, damned lies, and statistics."

6.50 In the first edition of this book the concluding section of chapter 6 contained a couple of pages of examples of how different sorts of financial calculation may go wrong if proper account is not taken of the effects of monetary inflation. It is no longer necessary to provide such a wide range of examples before drawing the moral that all measures of money have become systematically ambiguous. It was Aristotle who first drew attention to certain terms that have different meanings when applied to different sorts of things, yet the same meanings when applied to the same things. Our money measures now have a new variety of such systematic ambiguity: systematic ambiguity in the time dimension. The word for a dollar is the same word anywhere and at any one time. But a dollar (1997) is not, but is very much less than, a dollar (1947).

6.51 One consequence is that conscientious writers or speakers making financial comparisons across any period during which there has been substantial inflation in whatever currency they are employing as their means of measurement now always add parenthetic dates to the names of those currencies in order to indicate the real values. That is indeed a criterion of their conscientiousness.

7

A Chapter of Errors

7.1 It is a pity that chapter 6 had to stop when it did. Nothing but good could have come from examining more, and more various, ways in which figures can be misinterpreted. It is equally a pity that this chapter will again be far too short. In both cases the examination of more, and more various, examples is the practice that can scarcely fail to improve practice. Yet the first thing is to appreciate that what is needed most and all the time is an unspecialized critical alertness. We must always be ready to discern a fault in argument in any field, and most especially when that argument is our own or seems to support some conclusion we ourselves cherish. Both where figures are involved and more generally where they are not the faithful treatment of a few examples should be sufficient to emphasize the need and indicate the kind of discipline required in order to do better.

7.2 There is a fine tale, probably apocryphal, told of that notoriously merry British monarch Charles II. The story goes that there was a dinner to commemorate the foundation of the Royal Society of London, one of the great scientific institutions. At the end of the evening, "with that peculiar gravity of countenance which he usually wore on such occasions," he put a challenge to the Fellows: " 'Suppose two pails of water were fixed in two different scales that were equally poised, and which weighed equally alike, and that two live bream, or other small fish, were put into either of these pails,' he wanted to know the reason why that pail, with such additions, should not weigh more than the other pail which stood against it." Many suggested possible explanations and argued for their own suggestions with more or less vigor. But, at last, one, who perhaps remembered that the Latin motto of that society is "Nullius in verba" (Take no man's word for it!), denied the assumption: "It would weigh more." The king was delighted: "Odds fish, brother, you are in the right" (D'Israeli 1814, p. 341).

7.3 The king's move was an instance of what has traditionally been called the Fallacy of Many Questions. The stock example usually offered is the question, "When did you stop beating your wife?" when this is put to a man who either is not married at all, or else has not started, or perhaps has started but not stopped, beating his wife. It is not clear that what is wrong here is, in the strictest sense, a fallacy. But obviously it is wrong to build false assumptions into a question and to give answers that accept such assumptions. The mistake here—as in the case of the so-called Pathetic Fallacy (see paragraph 1.52)—is that of making unwarranted assumptions. The crux is noticed in chapter 6 of Caroll's *Alice's Adventures in Wonderland* (1865): " 'How am I to get in?' asked Alice again, in a louder tone. 'Are you to get in at all?' said the Footman. 'That's the first question, you know.' "

7.4 Unfortunately these, like all the best textbook illustrations, make it so clear what is going wrong that it may become hard to believe that anyone could make such a mistake seriously and ingenuously. But a crucial and contestable assumption may be very hard indeed to unearth when it is concealed in a longer and more complicated statement. Even when it is embodied in a single and lucid sentence we may well miss it. Consider, for instance, exchanges that may occur in national assemblies on the all-too-rare occasions on which the current administration proposes some reductions in direct personal taxation. Opponents may well complain that too much or too little is to be given away and/or that it is to be given to the wrong sets of taxpayers. Or consider an assertion made in what Ninian Smart believed to be a neutral and uncommitted study of *The Religious Experience of Mankind*: "We have records of the inaugural visions of some of the Old Testament prophets, of the experiences which taught them something profoundly important about God, and that spurred them on to teach men in his name" (Smart 1971, p. 22).

7.5 After what has been said earlier about the ambiguity of such expressions as "the income and wealth of the nation," "the national wealth," "Gross Domestic Product," and "Gross National Product" (see paragraphs 5.22–5.23), it is easy to appreciate what has to be said about utterances of the first of these two kinds. It is—unless we want to make some radical socialist assumption—that we ought in such contexts to talk not of giving away but of not taking in the first place. The assumption concealed in the second passage is built into the phrase "the experiences which taught them something profoundly important about God." By writing these words Smart implicitly, and presumably without becoming fully seized of this implication, claims religious knowledge in both the strong and the weak senses distinguished earlier (see paragraphs 5.20–5.21). For there is a decisive difference between, on the one hand, affirming that someone enjoyed or suffered such and such experiences, which led them to believe this, that, or the other and, on the other hand, while still affirming that the experiences occurred, also conceding that those consequent beliefs were in fact true. If the beliefs in question are religious and if you are supposed to be writing a detached essay on comparative religion, then you have no business either to assert or to imply any propositions of the latter sort, not even if you do believe, and maybe rightly, that they actually are true.

7.6 To appreciate fully what has just been said it is necessary to master a distinction between two senses of the word "experience." It is a distinction essential for epistemology, (i.e., the theory of knowledge). In the everyday philosophical layperson's sense of "experience," if we say that someone has had experience of cows or computers or whatever else then there is no question but that there are such entities for them to have experience of and to be familiar with. But the other sense of "experience" is altogether different. In this sense of "experience," to say that someone had or was the subject of an experience is precisely not to say or imply that the person was in some sort of cognitive contact with something existing altogether independently of their experience of it. To speak of someone's experience in this sense is to talk exclusively about how things felt or seemed to that someone. It is talk without prejudice to any questions about possible causes of that experiencing external to and independent of its subject. In the first sense of the word "experience" it refers to experience (objective) and in the second to experience (subjective). The problem for anyone writing about experience of God is to provide reliable criteria for distinguishing the merely subjective from the genuinely objective, if any. For as the incorrigible Thomas Hobbes remarked in chapter 23 of *Leviathan*: "If any man pretend to me that God hath spoken to him . . . immediately, and I make doubt of it, I cannot easily perceive what argument he can produce to oblige me to believe it. . . . For to say that God . . . hath spoken to him in a dream is no more than to say he dreamed that God spoke to him."

7.7 The use of the word "experience" in the subjective sense is very much a philosophers' use. So before proceeding to the next fallacy it is worth saying a little more about this philosophers' idea of experience. Anyone not interested should skip at once to paragraph 7.10. It is generally agreed that the modern period in philosophy began in 1637 with the publication in French by René Descartes of *A Discourse on the Method*. This *Discourse* consists of only six short parts. The first three are quietly preparatory and tell of how Descartes came to be meditating "in a room with a stove." Then, suddenly, in the first two paragraphs of Part 4, he makes an intellectually explosive presentation of the almost all-corroding Cartesian doubt. What follows next (paragraph 7.8) is crucial quotations from those two paragraphs of *A Discourse on the Method*. (Anyone wanting to read more argument about the arguments of Descartes and other great philosophers is referred to Flew 1989.)

7.8 "I do not know whether I ought to tell you of the first meditations in which I engaged there; for they are so metaphysical and so unusual that perhaps they will not be to everyone's taste. Yet at the same time if people are to be able to judge whether the foundations which I have laid are sufficiently firm I am in a way forced to speak of them. . . . I thought that I must . . . reject as if it were absolutely false everything about which I could suppose there was the least doubt, in order to see if after that there remained anything which I believed which was entirely indubitable. So, on the grounds that our senses sometimes deceive us, I wanted to suppose that there was not anything corresponding to what they make us imagine. And, because some men make mistakes in reasoning—even with regard to the simplest matters of geometry—and fall into fallacies, I judged that I was as much subject to error as anyone else, and I rejected as unsound all the reasonings which I had hitherto taken for demonstrations. Finally, taking account of the fact that all the same experiences which we have when we are awake can also come to us when we are asleep without there being one of them which is then veridical, I resolved to pretend that everything which had ever entered into my mind was no more veridical than the illusions of my dreams."

7.9 One of the first conclusions of these meditations of Descartes was, therefore, that he must take all his experience as being only experience (subjective). Or, rather, that he must take it all only in this way until and unless he can find some reliable means of identifying some of it as being what we have distinguished as experience (objective). The writings of Descartes have been enormously influential. Ever since the first publication of his *Discourse* all the leading figures in philosophy have recognized that they had or have somehow to come to terms with the challenge of Cartesian doubt. (It should be said, just as an aside, that the Cartesian conception of "the simplest matters of geometry" was probably not the same as yours or mine. For Descartes was also a major creative mathematician. His main mathematical achievement was to have developed coordinate geometry.)

7.10 The Fallacy of Many Questions is, as was noted earlier (see paragraphs 7.2–7.3), not strictly a fallacy, although the importance for thinking of noticing what if anything is tacitly presupposed not only by questions but also by statements cannot be overemphasized. The Genetic Fallacy really is a fallacy and consists in arguing that the antecedents of something must be the same as their fulfillment. It would be committed by anyone who argued, presumably in the context of an abortion debate, that a fetus, even from the moment of conception, must really be a person because it is going to become one. But the fallacy is more usually exemplified in supposedly debunking equations moving in the opposite direction, from the developed whatever it may be to the actual or supposed antecedent.

7.11 Consider a pair of books that were in their brief day both best-sellers. Both were written by Desmond Morris, a professional zoologist wishing to popularize his subject. My copy of *The Naked Ape* reveals that one reviewer described it as "brilliantly effective, cogently argued, very readable." Another agreed: "As with the title, the entire book is full of fresh perception." The delighted publishers hailed it as "wildly successful." To explain the title the author wrote: "There are one hundred and ninety-three living species of monkeys and apes. One hundred and ninety-two of them are covered with hair. The exception is the naked ape, self-named homo sapiens" (Morris 1968, p. 9).

7.12 Since several reviewers went out of their way to praise that title, it is just worth pointing out that the opposites of "naked" and "covered with hair" are, respectively, "clothed" and "hairless." So any "fresh perception" here has resulted in a misdescription. It is, however, a misdescription that suits the author's purpose. This is metaphorically to strip man and, as he was to express it in a sequel, *The Human Zoo*, to reveal "a human animal, a primitive tribal hunter, masquerading as a civilized, supertribal citizen" (Morris 1970, p. 248). Certainly it can be salutary to be reminded that, whatever else we are or may become, we remain animals: "Even a space ape must urinate" (Morris 1968, p. 21). And certainly it is useful to insist that as animals we have inescapable problems generated by our fertility. But simply to identify us with our nearest ancestors on the evolutionary family tree is an altogether different thing. It is this which, again and again, Morris does: "Behind the facade of modern city life there is the same old naked ape. Only the names have been changed: for 'hunting' read 'working,' for 'home base' read 'house,' for 'pair bond' read 'marriage,' for 'mate' read 'wife,' and so on" (ibid., p. 74). Once more: "When you put your name on the door, or hang a painting on a wall, you are, in dog or wolf terms, for example, simply cocking your leg on them and leaving your personal mark there" (ibid., p. 161).

7.13 The nerve of the argument, and it is an argument that comes up all the time and all over the place, is that if this evolved from that, then this must always be that or at least it must always be really or essentially that. Yet a moment's thought shows that this argument is absurd. For to say that this evolved from that implies that this is different from that, and not the same. It is therefore peculiarly preposterous to offer as the fruit of evolutionary insight a systematic development of the thesis that we are what our ancestors were. Oaks are not, though they grow from, acorns; and—for better or for worse—civilized people are not, though they evolved from, apes.

7.14 Furthermore, it is also egregiously preposterous to present as biological understanding a wholesale depreciation of environment as opposed to heredity, of what is learned as opposed to what is instinctual. Certainly the distances between man and the brutes and between city folk and primitive people are in this perverse perspective narrowed. But it conceals what is a most distinctive and powerful peculiarity of our species, as compared with all others. This concealment is a very queer thing to parade as a zoologist's revelation.

7.15 The peculiarity is our comparatively enormous capacity for learning and the length of the period of the upbringing of children. This learning capacity, and its main trophy and instrument, language, provides our most favored species with an excellent substitute for the inheritance of acquired characteristics. I am especially happy to acknowledge that this is a point I myself first took from reading the essay on "Biology and Sociology" in Julian Huxley's *Essays of a Biologist* (1923). For this was a fine work of popularization, which demonstrated that to achieve popularity it is not necessary to sensationalize your subject by standing it on its head.

7.16 Before leaving the subject of the Genetic Fallacy a word needs to be said about *The Selfish Gene* (1976) by Richard Dawkins. This was his first book. It was written before *The Blind Watchmaker* (1986), his incomparably illuminating account of the process of biological evolution. The trouble with *The Selfish Gene* precisely is its title. For genes are not human beings, members of a kind of creatures that can and therefore cannot but make choices (Flew 1995, passim). To describe genes as selfish, therefore, is to commit a kind of Genetic Fallacy, the kind that proceeds from the more developed whatever it may be to the actual or supposed antecedent of that more developed whatever it may be. Even to describe genes as self-interested, which is the opposite of disinterested, is at least awkward and misleading. For that contrast, like the contrasts between being selfish, being unselfish, and not being remarkably either, is one we can apply comfortably, if at all, only to ourselves and our fellow human beings, creatures of a kind that can, and therefore cannot but, make choices (see paragraphs 3.13–3.14).

7.17 The temptation to commit the Genetic Fallacy is greater when the evolution is thought to have been smoothly continuous. For it is then reinforced by the different temptations of the Logically-black-is-white Slide. This unsound form of argument is extremely popular, although it is rarely made fully explicit. It runs roughly as follows: "The difference we are dealing with is a difference of degree. Since with such a difference there can be no natural break at which a sharp line of division is, as it were, already drawn, there can be no logical stopping place on any journey from one extreme to the other. The difference cannot, therefore, be one of either kind or principle. So it must really be either nonexistent or, at best, unimportant."

7.18 The first thing is to get a little clearer about differences of degree. Let us say that a difference of degree between two extremes is one such that there is or could be a series of actual cases, or theoretically possible cases, stretching between one of these extremes and the other, and with the amount of difference between each member of the series and the next vanishingly small. It becomes obvious that in any such series "there can be no natural break at which a sharp line of division is, as it were, already drawn."

7.19 But it should also be obvious that differences that are both large and in this sense differences of degree can be of the last importance. For the differences between age and youth, between riches and poverty, between sanity and insanity, between a free society and one in which everything not forbidden is compulsory, are all paradigm cases of large differences that are differences of degree in the sense just now explicated. It must therefore be as wrong as it surely is common to move as if no move had been made and, hence, without any particular justification, from saying that this is a difference of degree to saying that this is a *mere* difference of degree.

7.20 What starts people down the disastrous Logically-black-is-white Slide is the observation that some difference is a difference of degree, and that "there can be no natural break at which a sharp line of division is, as it were, already drawn." This is, as we have just seen (see paragraph 7.18), a defining characteristic of differences of degree. What is wrong is to assume that it warrants the conclusion that even the largest of such differences "must really be either nonexistent or, at best, unimportant." It is possible to disentangle, a little artificially, three separate strands in this error.

7.21 First is the notion that, if a distance is one which is or could be traveled in a series of very short steps, then it cannot even in sum amount to much: a muckle cannot be made of no matter how many mickles. This wretched misconception has a classical label. It is called either *The Sorites* (Greek, pronounced So-wry-tees) or *The Heaper*: "Since a single grain of sand does not make a heap, and since adding one more is at no stage enough to convert what we have into a heap, there cannot really be heaps."

7.22 Second is the idea that we cannot properly distinguish between this and that, much less insist that the difference is desperately important, unless we are able to draw a sharp line between one and the other. Of course the lack of such a line may sometimes be very inconvenient. Still it does not even begin to show that when the items distinguished are well clear of the undemarcated no man's land, we cannot or should not make such distinctions. As Edmund Burke, with his usual good sense, once said: "[T]hough no man can draw a stroke between the confines of night and day, still light and darkness are on the whole tolerably distinguishable."

7.23 Third is the assumption that where there is no obvious natural break, and hence where any line drawn must be artificially drawn, there both our drawing of any line and our decision to draw that line at one particular point rather than another must be illogical. These are the most important misconceptions. They nevertheless are misconceptions.

7.24 Here we should recall what was said earlier (see paragraphs 1.31–1.37) about the reasons why logic sometimes gets a bad press. The second of these was "that it is confused with various things that have nothing to do with it" (see paragraph 1.35). There certainly is nothing logical, in our primary sense, about impractical practices or unworkable institutions. One source of trouble is that the logical may be contrasted either with the illogical or with the neither logical nor illogical. The

rational may similarly be contrasted with either the irrational or the neither rational or irrational. The correct interpretation of the words "logical" and "rational" must depend on what is in the context the appropriate contrast. Furthermore, as we have just noticed in discussing *The
Selfish Gene* (see paragraph 7.16), not only are there innumerable sorts
of objects of discourse that cannot properly be characterized as either
selfish or unselfish, there are also even actions that neither merit praise
as unselfish nor deserve blame as selfish (see paragraphs 3.13–3.14). So
it is in discussion often both helpful and to the point to press what might
be dubbed Is-there-a-third-way Questions. One of these is the question
whether one of the pair of contrasting terms in the dispute in question is
one of another pair in another relevant contrast. The other is the question whether the two terms in the dispute are not only mutually exclusive but also together exhaustive.

7.25 We noticed the two possible contrasts with the rational when
earlier (see paragraphs 4.7–4.8) we disposed of the unsound argument
that if there are always physiological causes of my uttering the sounds I
utter, then I cannot have and know that I have good reasons for believing
the propositions I assert by uttering those words. The unsound argument
is that if it is the one, then it must be merely that and not the other also.
The point there is that these physiological causes should have been
described not as irrational but as nonrational. When Aristotle, centuries
before we could be picked out as members of the species *homo sapiens*,
defined man as the rational animal he was not—as Bertrand Russell and
others have sometimes mischievously suggested—loftily ignoring the
irrationality of all of us some of the time and of some of us a great deal
of the time. Instead, what Aristotle was doing was picking out what
seemed to him the most important, the most remarkable distinguishing
characteristic of our species, namely, that we are all at least potentially
rational and hence also potentially irrational.

7.26 Aristotle was here making a point that runs parallel with the
one that would be made by anyone defining human beings as moral animals, namely, that we are at least potentially moral and hence, and necessarily, potentially immoral. In both cases the possibility of striving to
reach the ideal necessarily presupposes and is presupposed by the possibility of defection from it. For both rationality and irrationality,

morality and immorality, are possible only for members of a kind of creatures that can and therefore cannot but make choices and that are
always or almost always able to do and to think in ways other than those
in which they do do and do think (Flew 1995, chapter 6).

7.27 We have been insisting that it is a mistake to take it that what
is neither logical nor illogical, neither rational nor irrational—what we
have been describing as the nonlogical and the nonrational—has to be
by the same token illogical, or irrational. It is also a dangerous mistake.
For it encourages all those who value some things which are nonlogical,
or nonrational—as, hopefully, we all do—invalidly to infer that these
humanly indispensable values militate against, or even preclude, logic
and rationality. Certainly there is a place in life for passion, for compassion, and for commitment. For the illogical and the irrational there
is, or ought to be, none.

7.28 Descending from the rather abstract and theoretical level of the
previous few paragraphs and considering some of the paradigm cases of
differences of degree already mentioned, it is easy to see that we often
have the most excellent reasons for drawing a line. Suppose we want to
mount a round-the-clock operation. Then we shall need to fix some pretty
precise point in the diurnal cycle at which the day watch is to take over
from the night watch, or the day shift from the night shift. Suppose there
is to be a speed limit. Then a line has to be drawn between those speeds
that are to be legally permissible and those that are not. If certain legal
rights and duties are to be attached to adult status, then it becomes practically essential to determine some moment in people's lives when they
become legally adult. And so on. There is absolutely nothing illogical
about being led by such practical considerations to draw sharp lines,
lines which necessarily are, in the sense explained (see paragraph 7.18),
artificial. And, furthermore, since the choice to do this is reasoned, it is
diametrically wrong to berate it as arbitrary.

7.29 There may also be, and again there often are, good reasons
why the line to be drawn should be drawn through this particular point
rather than that, or at least good reasons why it should be drawn through
one of the points of this particular sort rather than through any of the
rest. For instance, given that we have some standard units for measuring

the difference in question, then everyone will find it easier, more natural as opposed to forced, if any line that is to be socially important—not to say socially divisive—is drawn through some point corresponding to a whole and preferably a round number of these standard units. Even though the choice between 18 or 19 or 10 or 21 as the age of majority may have to be unreasoned and hence arbitrary, the decisions to fix some age of majority, and to fix it so that the line is drawn at a birthday rather than at any other day in the year are by no means unreasoned and, hence, not arbitrary.

7.30 Whatever artificial dividing lines we draw across any differences of degree are bound to generate paradoxes of the little more and how much it is, and of the little less and how little: "If only Jack had been born an hour sooner he would not have been caught by the draft, and if only Jill had breasted the tape a split second sooner she would have established a new world record." The argument may then be offered that so much ought not to hinge upon these so littles. To this the only but sufficient general reply is to insist that just because so many humanly vital differences are differences of degree and just because for the best of reasons we do have to draw artificial lines of division across these continuous differences, the occurrence of some such paradoxes, with all the consequent heartburn and self-congratulation, is an inescapable part of the human condition.

7.31 What we must on no account do, once such lines have been established, is to pretend that the particular little more or little less is all that is now in jeopardy. For the line laid down was a line of policy, and in that sense of principle. So what is now in question is not only that particular little more or little less, but also, for better or for worse, the general policy or principle that any breach must challenge. For instance, if the frontier line between two states is drawn across a desert, then an incursion a few miles deep by the forces of one or the other will not—if the possibility of finding oil is precluded—result in either an intrinsically worthwhile gain for the incursor or an intrinsically substantial loss for the victim of the incursion. But, if the victim state were simply to ignore what the other state had done, then by failing to make any response at all it would have both sacrificed the principle of its own territorial integrity and made it more difficult to establish and maintain a fresh and firmer line of resistance if it decided in the future that establishing such a line of resistance was what it wanted to do.

7.32 So far none of our illustrations has been drawn from commercial advertising. In some circles so much is urged or assumed about the alleged evils of this activity that the absence of such illustrations may strike many readers as curious. But it becomes less surprising when we consider how small a proportion of such advertising output is argumentative prose. The case would of course be very different if we were to bring into account the advertising of politicians. Certainly when I checked through the commercial advertisements printed in the journals which come regularly into our house, and paid more attention than usual to those other advertisements that interrupt the television programs I watch, I found that I was able to distinguish two chief kinds of advertising material. One kind attempts to associate the products advertised with people, places, and activities who or which the advertisers believe that their target public will find attractive. Nothing needs to be said about this here. The other kind provides information about the product. Such information is in the First World and with widely advertised products rarely, if ever, straightforwardly false. This is because the provision of indisputably false information about their products is usually both illegal and against the longer-term interests of the advertisers themselves. For they cannot hope to continue to achieve good sales for their products in any market in which it becomes known that they have been dishonestly promoting those products.

7.33 Naturally the information given by advertisers will, where there are alternatives, be presented in a way favorable to the interests of the advertisers. For example, consider an advertisement for beer. There is a difference, which is not a difference in the amount or the accuracy of the information given about the beer, between saying that the mug is already half empty and saying that it is still half full. My own two favorite examples of such accentuation of the positive are, perhaps fittingly, both drawn from the United States. In response to distress about the environmental effects of phosphates one wide-awake firm spread the exultant sales message that its domestic detergent was "98.8 percent phosphate free." The Atomic Energy Commission (AEC) also rapidly became most careful to promote what used to be called Hazard Analyses as, more encouragingly, Safety Analyses.

7.34 More serious, and of more obvious concern to us here, are certain other ways of putting a better face on percentages and similar quantitative comparisons. The first and most fundamental question to ask about all percentages is "percentage of what?" As we emphasized in chapter 6, 70 percent of those now in Ruritania's jails is not at all the same thing as 70 percent of all Ruritania's first offenders (see paragraphs 6.1–6.3). The news that profits in retailing have increased or are to be by law reduced by 10 percent tells us nothing in particular until we know whether this is a percentage of mark-up over wholesale prices or of gross profits on capital employed. It is the former that directly determines prices in the shops. But that is very different from, and is almost bound to be enormously larger than, the latter, since it is from the former that retailers have to meet all their costs—premises, wages, equipment, and so on.

7.35 Suppose you boast that the New Splodge contains 50 percent more of some supposedly gorgeous ingredient. Then your boast is as near as makes no matter completely empty if no one else knows, and you are not telling, how much there was in it before. Such no doubt true statements can be doubly misleading thanks to certain very simple mathematical properties of percentages. The birth of a woman's second child constituted a 100 percent increase in her family, whereas if she were to have a fifth child, that one would represent only a 25 percent addition to her previous four. And if a man were to suffer a 50 percent cut in anything, he would then need a 100 percent increase to get back to where he was before the cut.

7.36 Other simple mathematical properties are important in the pictorial representation of data comparisons. The area of any plane figure, if the shape is held constant, increases much faster than any of its dimensions. In the simplest case, that of the square, the doubling of the length of the sides quadruples the area. It will not do, therefore, to represent the gratifying rise in the sales of electric toasters by a series of undistorted pictures of toasters, one for each year, in which the sales figures correlate with the height or the width of the sketches. For the increases in the areas of these sketches must then be far greater than the sales increases they purport to illustrate. There is a similar disparity between the increase in the area of a square and the growth in the volume of the corresponding cube. It may be helpful as a mnemonic to remark that it was part of the genius of Isambard Kingdom Brunel, who in 1838 built the first steamship to make transatlantic trips, to see the relevance of this to the problem of building a coal-fired steamship capable of carrying itself, its crew, and a profitable payload across the Atlantic. The relevance is "that whereas the carrying capacity of a hull increases as the cube of its dimensions, its resistance, or in other words the power required to drive it through the water, only increases as the square of those dimensions" (Rolt 1957, p. 249).

7.37 Mistakes and misdemeanors exploiting these and other simple mathematical properties certainly are to be found in commercial advertisements, as well as perhaps even more commonly in other, noncommercial forms of publicity. Then again one might, I suppose, deem as a sort of arguments all the attempts made by salespersons to build up favorable associations for their products. If so, then it is certainly a bad sort of arguments for buying those products. But to talk in this way surely is to stretch the word "argument" a bit too far to be helpful? And anyway, if, as is often the case with the different brands competing in mature markets, there is precious little if any difference in either quality or price between one brand and another, then it is hard to think of any reason for choosing one particular brand other than that you simply find its advertising more appealing than that of the competition.

7.38 I can offer from the earliest pages of my private philosophical scrapbook a prize specimen of one kind of bad reason that can be found not only in commercial advertisements but also in many other contexts. This specimen came from an advertisement for a substance called Silvikrin. The advertisement was published in the long-since-defunct British weekly *Picture Post*, a journal that had been modeled on the also-long-defunct but since resurrected American weekly *Life*. Under the heading "Can baldness be postponed?" we read: "Faced with fast-falling hair most people make some attempt to delay the evil day when baldness can no longer be denied. Some try to disguise the fact with long forelocks and other subterfuges. But the wise and knowledgeable face up to the fact that their hair is dying from 'natural causes' and that a *natural treatment* is the only hope of saving the situation" (September 9, 1950, emphasis original).

7.39 Does this argument really have any more force than the contention that he who drives fat oxen must himself be fat? As we shall soon be seeing (see paragraph 7.42), there certainly is something more to the natural than there is to fatness. And many of the people who would at once recognize that the second contention has no force at all would hesitate to dismiss so immediately the argument about natural causes and natural treatments. Certainly we do not have to wait long before we come across someone arguing that because something is natural it must therefore be as it ideally ought to be. Such people could easily be persuaded to agree that "Nature knows best" (Commoner 1972, p. 37). Once the form of such arguments is clearly spelled out, however, it becomes obvious that the arguments are fallacious. For they proceed from what as a pure and simple matter of brute fact is allegedly the case directly to the conclusion that what thus is the case is as things ideally ought to be. This fallacy of moving directly from *is* to *ought* has a name: the Naturalistic Fallacy.

7.40 Its nature was classically expounded by David Hume in a very characteristic paragraph of *A Treatise of Human Nature* (1739–40). This paragraph is worth quoting in full as a fine example of good eighteenth-century English prose. But readers need to be warned that what Hume claims to have observed in writings about "systems of morality" is not really what the authors actually did write and what he actually did read. Rather, it is what the authors should have written and what they would have written if only they had properly appreciated the structure of their own arguments. For even the best of writers and thinkers may sometimes, without noticing the significance of what they are doing, slide from employing words such as "natural" and "normal" in their *is* senses into using them in *ought* senses. For instance, they start by first noticing that some sort of behaviors is normal—meaning that, for better or for worse, most people do usually behave in such a manner. They then proceed without further argument to the conclusion that such behavior is normal—meaning here and now that it consists with appropriate prescribed moral or other norms. Paragraph 7.41 is thus a verbatim quotation of that famous paragraph from the *Treatise* (III[i]2), preserving all the original spellings and punctuations.

7.41 "I cannot forbear adding to these reasonings an observation which may, perhaps, be found of some importance. In every system of morality, which I have hitherto met with, I have always remark'd, that the author proceeds for some time in the ordinary way of reasoning, and establishes the being of a God, or makes observations concerning human affairs; when of a sudden I am surpriz'd to find, that instead of the usual copulations of propositions, *is*, and *is not*, I meet with no proposition that is not connected with an *ought*, and an *ought not*. This change is imperceptible; but is, however, of the last consequence. For as this *ought*, or *ought not*, expresses some new relation or affirmation, 'tis necessary that it shou'd be observ'd and explain'd; and at the same time that a reason should be given, for what seems altogether inconceivable, how this new relation can be deduction from others, which are entirely different from it. But as authors do not commonly use this precaution, I shall presume to recommend it to the readers; and am persuaded, that this small attention wou'd subvert all the vulgar systems of morality, and let us see, that the distinction of vice and virtue is not founded merely on the relations of objects, nor is perceiv'd by reason" (III[i]2).

7.42 The "something more to the natural than there is to fatness," that is, the something which leads some people to believe that "Nature knows best," perhaps is or involves some sort of personification of Nature as a benevolent deity. Given that sort of belief, it becomes not altogether irrational for one to believe, as biologist disaster prophet Barry Commoner seems to have done, that whereas all naturally produced chemical compounds are harmless, all those artificially produced are likely to be in some way dangerous if not positively poisonous. These consequent beliefs are all known to be false. For instance, there are, and have been for millions of years before the origin of our particular species, numerous naturally produced carcinogens—substances capable in sufficient quantities of generating cancers (Efron 1984, pp. 136–37 and passim).

7.43 Anyone who wants to discuss carcinogens or any other kind of poisons sensibly needs to know that every kind of substance both natural and artificial is in some quantity poisonous, and also that particular quantities that are not poisonous to one species may be very poisonous to another. The fundamental principle of toxicology was famously stated by the sixteenth-century German physician known as Paracelsus: "What is it that is not poison? All things are poison and none is without poison. Only the dose determines that a thing is not poison" (quoted in Efron 1984, p. 144). That is why the not-one-molecule policy of zero tolerance for supposed carcinogens—a policy which was at one time very vigorously promoted, especially in the United States—was impractical and absurd.

7.44 Although a policy of zero tolerance for supposed carcinogens makes no sense in a war on cancer, it may be, and in New York it apparently has been, remarkably effective in the war on crime. With regard to the latter kind of war there are always those eager to tell us that we cannot hope for much success until and unless we succeed in removing some or all of the supposed root causes for crime. Chief Justice Earl Warren, for instance, found crime "in our disturbed society" to be due to "root causes" such as "slum life in the ghettos, ignorance, [and] poverty" (Warren 1977, p. 317). Such claims are rarely, if ever, supported by statistics showing correlations between, on the one hand, increases or decreases in the amounts of crime and, on the other hand, increases or decreases in the numbers of people living in slums and in ignorance and poverty. Indeed the people who issue these pronouncements seem to be among those who, as the Nobel laureate George Stigler so characteristically put it, "issue stern ultimata to the public on almost a monthly basis, and sometimes on no other basis" (quoted in Sowell 1993, p. 72).

7.45 Here we are concerned with the question of what is meant and implied by saying that something is a root cause of crime, rather than with the question of whether any such hypothesis about the root causes of crime is actually true. If anyone does wish to pursue the latter question they would be well advised to consult Dennis 1997. For this work shows very clearly that in the United Kingdom the relation between the crime statistics and the statistics showing the strength of the supposed root causes is more nearly inverse than direct. But to appreciate what is meant and implied by talk about the supposed root causes of crime we need first to make a fundamental distinction between two senses of the word "cause."

7.46 When we are talking about the causes of some purely physical event—an eclipse of the sun, say—then we employ the word "cause" in a sense implying both physical necessity and physical impossibility: What happened was physically necessary and, under the circumstances, anything else was physically impossible. Yet this is precisely not the case with the other sense of "cause," the sense in which we speak of the causes of human actions. For instance, if I give someone good cause to celebrate, I do not hereby make it inevitable that the person will celebrate. To adapt a famous phrase from the German philosopher mathematician Gottfried Leibniz (1646–1716), causes of this second, personal sort incline but do not necessitate. So it remains entirely up to the individual whether or not to celebrate.

7.47 Hume appears to have been the first to make this distinction clearly and sharply. In his essay "Of National Characters" he wrote: "By *moral* causes, I mean all circumstances, which are fitted to work on the mind as motives or reasons. . . . By *physical* causes I mean those qualities of the air and climate, which are supposed to work insensibly on the temper, by altering the tone and habit of the body . . ." (Hume 1985, p. 198). Because Hume denied the reality of physical necessity, he could not make this distinction quite as we have done. But his choice of labels for the two senses distinguished does indicate a fundamental difference between, on the one hand, the natural sciences and, on the other hand, the social, or as he and his contemporaries would have said, the moral sciences.

7.48 Once we apply this distinction between two senses of "cause" to assertions about supposed root causes of crime, there can be little doubt but that those who so confidently make these assertions would want them to be interpreted as necessitating (physical) rather than as merely motivating (moral) causes. For what otherwise would be the radical and challenging novelty in such assertions? Surely no one would wish to deny that poverty, ignorance, and slum conditions generally can provide very strong temptations to take criminal actions and that those who have been convicted of committing crimes may in consequence sometimes very reasonably appeal to those things as extenuating or even totally excusing circumstances. That none of these temptation-generating conditions constitutes an always necessitating cause of crime can be established by referring to the fact that by no means all those people who are subject to them become criminals. (For further discussion of this distinction between two senses of "cause," see Flew 1995, pp.

122–47. For a now somewhat dated introduction to the problems of crime in the United States, see Wilson 1975. For what has some claim to constitute the comprehensive and definitive study of crime and human nature, see Wilson and Herrnstein 1985.)

7.49 Somewhat similar to the claim that certain unfortunate conditions are the root causes of crime is the claim that society is to blame. For instance, it has been vehemently said that "Everyone is learning how to cop out of personal responsibility by blaming 'society.' From teenagers in high school to hardened felons in prison, they can tell you how the traumas they were put through by 'society' caused everything from failing grades to armed robbery. People who would rather mooch than work used to be called bums, but now they are homeless 'victims' of 'society' " (Sowell 1987, p. 232).

7.50 If we are reasonably either to accept or to reject such claims, then we need first to persuade those who make them to explain what they mean by them and how and by whom the responsibility for whatever defect is in question was supposedly incurred. It seems likely that we shall have difficulty in securing any satisfactory answer to these questions. While Margaret Thatcher was prime minister of the United Kingdom she once, in an interview with the weekly *Woman's Own* of October 31, 1987, confessed: "I don't believe in Society. There is no such thing, only individual people, and there are families."

7.51 To my mind this entirely innocuous utterance, usually misreported as being simply "There is no such thing as society," generated an extraordinarily widespread and sustained uproar. For instance, I myself have met in the columns of quarterly journals published in the United States and Australia years after she was ejected from the prime ministership, angry denunciations of Margaret Thatcher for not believing in the existence of society. But I have never at any time succeeded in persuading any such denouncers to explain what it was they held to be true and believed that she had denied.

7.52 Certainly it is possible to say sensible things about society, and some of these things are extremely important. For instance, Thomas Hobbes wrote in his *De Cive (The Citizen)* (1642) that "civil societies are not mere meetings, but bonds, to the making whereof faith and compacts are necessary; the virtue whereof to children and fools, and the profit whereof to those who have not yet tasted the miseries that accompany its defects, is altogether unknown; whence it happens that those, who know not what society is, cannot enter it; those because ignorant of the benefit it brings, care not for it."

7.53 All this is indeed both true and important. But it still provides us with no reason for believing that a society consists of anything in addition to the individuals and/or the families of which it is composed. And it is only these individuals and/or sometimes the individual members of the government of that society, if it has one, who can properly be held responsible and praised or blamed for what they have done or failed to do. We might most illuminatingly say of a society or nation or nation-state what was once famously said of history: "History does *nothing*; it 'does not possess immense riches,' it 'does *not* fight battles.' It is not 'history' which uses men as a means of achieving—as if it were an individual person—its *own* ends. History is nothing but the activity of men in pursuit of their ends" (Marx and Engels 1845, p. 93, emphasis original).

7.54 So to the offenders who say, or, more often, to the offenders of whom others say, that not they but society is to blame for their offenses, we have to insist that for every individual person society is and can only be everyone else but that person. So if any offenders are to be shown not to have been truly responsible for committing their offenses, it must be up to either them or their presumably nonoffending defenders to try to show either that it was not the offenders themselves but some other particular individuals who were really responsible for the offenders committing the offenses formerly attributed to them; or that the offenders' social situation was such that they could not reasonably have been expected (prescriptive) not to have committed those offenses.

7.55 I refuse to conclude this chapter without sharing another commercial item from my philosophical scrapbook. Let it serve as a final cheerful reinforcement for what was said earlier about the crucial importance of contradiction and noncontradiction (see paragraphs 1.10–1.31). This item comes from a circular letter from Dover Publications, a New York firm with a very useful line of reprints of classical texts in philosophy, science, and—wait for it!—logic. It reads: "We shall enjoy hearing from you, and for your convenience we are enclosing a business reply envelope which requires no postage (due to U.S. postal regulations reply envelopes cannot be used from foreign addresses, and therefore none is enclosed)."

8

The Final Foreword

8.1 Insofar as any book of the present sort is successful, its end must be a new beginning. Yet for many the effect of appreciating some of the great variety of mistakes that can be made in reasoning may be not encouragement, but despair. Surely it must be practically impossible to avoid all these and other mistakes and to get everything right? No doubt it is. But it is as wrong here as it is everywhere else to argue that if I cannot do everything, then I cannot, and am not obliged to, do anything. For instance, it is intellectually, but not only intellectually, shabby to argue that because I cannot contribute either money or time and effort to all the causes which may make demands on me, therefore I cannot and need not contribute to any. It is also an error, albeit one committed by the great Immanuel Kant himself, to contend that striving after perfection must presuppose a commitment to the belief that actual perfection can and perhaps will be achieved.

8.2 Perhaps the shortness of the book will reduce such temptations to discouragement. Wise teachers keep their reading lists short partly lest their students should conclude that because they cannot read everything they do not need to read anything. But the main thing to stress again now is that the challenge to think better is a challenge to our integrity.

137

8.3 Chapter 1 tried to bring out how the notion of valid deductive argument is and must be defined in terms of contradiction and noncontradiction (see paragraphs 1.1–1.10). No one who has any concern with what is or is not true can afford to be unmoved by the threat or still more by the actuality of self-contradiction (see paragraphs 1.16–1.26). Chapter 2 revealed the essentially hypothetical character of valid argument. It is argued, if such and such a proposition is true then it follows that, and we may validly deduce that, some other proposition is also true. But—and this is of crucial importance for scientific enquiry—whereas the truth of such a validly drawn deduction does not guarantee the truth of the premise from which it is thus validly deduced, its falsity does decisively demonstrate the falsity of that premise. The same chapter developed the distinctions between, on the one hand, logically necessary and logically sufficient conditions and, on the other hand, causally necessary and causally sufficient conditions (see paragraphs 2.18–2.29). It also distinguished the concept of the contrary from that of the contradictory (see paragraphs 2.37–2.40).

8.4 Chapter 3 displayed some of the possibilities of deceiving ourselves by making covert shifts between substantial and merely tautological interpretations of the same forms of words (see paragraphs 3.1–3.10). The same chapter then went on to link this with the Popperian thesis that a forthright concern for truth demands an emphasis upon the possibilities of falsification and a permanent critical openness toward their realization (see paragraphs 3.17–3.26).

8.5 In chapter 4 the main concern was to insist that any insights we have into the reasons why people may be inclined to hold or to utter certain propositions (whether these reasons are motives or causes) and any insights we may gain from the future advancement of psychology and sociology should be harnessed to the improvement of our thinking. They should not be misemployed to distract attention from questions about the reasons (grounds) for holding that these propositions are true or, as the case may be, false (see paragraphs 4.3–4.28). Then in chapter 5 it was urged that to play Humpty Dumpty with the established meanings of words is to act in bad faith (see paragraphs 5.32–5.35).

8.6 It is time at least to suggest a wider connection between rationality in general and personal integrity. This suggestion is the more important and the more timely because it is nowadays fashionable to disdain the former, and in particular the exacting standards of science, in favor of a supposedly incompatible ideal of sincerity in personal relationships. This is a preposterous antithesis, since sincerity and integrity require what is being in their name rejected.

8.7 In chapter 1 I wrote: "To say that someone knows something is to say more than that he claims to know it or that he believes it most strongly. It is to say also both that it is true and that he is in a position to know that it is true. So neither the sincerity of his conviction nor the ingenuousness of his utterance guarantees that he really knew" (see paragraph 1.57). Someone may be absolutely sincere and ingenuous in claiming to know, and yet nevertheless turn out to have been mistaken. That this can and does happen is both a philosophical and an everyday commonplace.

8.8 What is not quite so often remarked is that to the extent that I make claims to knowledge without ensuring that I am indeed in a position to know, I must prejudice my claims both to sincerity and to ingenuousness. It is just not honest for me to pretend to know the winners of tomorrow's greyhound races when I am not directly or indirectly acquainted with either the form of the dogs or the plans of the dopers. Nor will my dishonesty be diminished— though the consequent damage will be—if my predictions happen to be fulfilled. Notwithstanding that law cannot be equated with morals, nor belief with knowledge, it is to the point to notice that, by the U.K. Perjury Act of 1911, it is perjury to swear what we believe to be false, regardless of whether what we swore to happened to be true (Stephen 1950, vol. 4, p. 148). No doubt many other jurisdictions make similar provisions. Compare, for instance, the words of Abraham Lincoln as quoted in paragraph 1.18.

8.9 Being in a position to know is not always or even most often a matter of being able to deduce what is known from premises also known. Clearly it could not be. For on this assumption knowledge would be impossible since it would require the completion of an infinite series of deductions from premises all of which would have first to be deduced from others, in turn first deduced from others, and so on. Sometimes we know without inference, as when we know that something hurts or that there is a great big truck right in front of our eyes. Where the need for rational appraisal has to enter is in the determination that we are indeed in a position to know and do know. This need becomes urgent whenever there are grounds for fearing that we may be mistaken. For to maintain any belief while dismissing, or refusing to give due weight to, reasonable and relevant objections is to show that you are more concerned to maintain that belief than really to know whether it or something else is, after all, true.

8.10 Something similar holds, too, with regard to policies and programs. Suppose we propose some policy or support some program on the grounds that its implementation will lead to various shining results. Then we have to accept that to precisely the extent that we are genuinely and sincerely devoted to those splendid objectives, we shall be eager to monitor the actual results of implementation and ready to make or to support some appropriate change of course the moment that it emerges, if it does, that we were mistaken in thinking that these policies would fulfill our original aspirations.

8.11 Suppose that we are not in this way ready and eager to learn from our mistakes. Then we make it cruelly clear that our true concern either always was, or has now become, not concern for the stated objectives of our policy or program, but concern for something else altogether. Perhaps our real object never was what we said it was. Or perhaps our pride and other sentiments have become involved in that program. Perhaps it was our personal program and/or the program of a party to which we are strongly attached. The actual implementation of that program thus becomes for us not a means to the realization of its originally stated objectives but an end in itself.

8.12 As the matter has been put in the previous two paragraphs, the necessary connections between sincerity of purpose, rationality, and an insistence upon monitoring success or failure in achieving that purpose must seem obvious and undeniable. Surely no one with any pretensions to rationality could fail to see these connections and act appropriately? But the truth is almost the contrary (see paragraphs 2.37–2.40). Almost no one promoting or engaged in the implementation of public policies seems to see these connections and act appropriately; unless, that is, you count as appropriate action on the part of those who have their own unpublicized reasons for keeping secret the actual effects of implementing the policy in question, the inaction of not supporting or demanding monitoring.

8.13 Since I do not want to seem to be taking sides in any current U.S. controversy I will now draw a vividly scandalous example from a book published in Beverly Hills and London eighteen years ago (Price et al. 1980). It was announced as the first of a series of *Annual Reviews of Community Mental Health*. What then called itself the "community mental health movement" in the United States consisted of all—as its members certainly would have wished us to say—person programs launched under the Community Mental Health Centers Act of 1963. This was passed in response to a presidential message to the Congress on "Mental Health and Mental Retardation," dated February 5, 1963. President Kennedy, who had a particular family reason for being especially concerned about this subject, made it absolutely clear what were the good results which were desired. Demanding "a bold new approach" he emphasized that "prevention is far more desirable for all concerned" than cure. Without specifying any illustrative examples, he called for "selective specific programs directed at known causes."

8.14 Fifteen or more years later a collective of contributors, all of whom are members of this movement and who therefore have strong and obvious personal stakes in the continuation and expansion of these programs, published this *Annual Review*. Judging by the contents, and still more by what it does not contain, no one expected it to be studied by any critical outsider. For with this book—as with Sherlock Holmes and the dog not barking during the night—the most remarkable thing is what does not happen. Nowhere from beginning to end does there occur one single reference, whether direct or indirect, to any evidence that any of these programs has actually succeeded in reducing the incidence of mental retardation or mental illness or even in holding it down below the higher level to which it might perhaps otherwise have been expected to rise.

8.15 Had there in fact been any such demonstrated successes, we can be sure that this book would have been full of allusions to them. Furthermore, everyone who had joined and was remaining in "the movement" with the prime intention of helping to prevent or cure such manifestly evil afflictions would have been rejoicing in the successes already achieved, while anyone proposing fresh initiatives toward similar ends would have been eager to learn and to apply the lessons to be drawn from those past achievements. The unlovely truth, however, was otherwise. These proud "prevention professionals," professing carers and compassionists though they were, did not, it seems, feel constrained even to pretend to have fulfilled any part of the beneficent (do-gooding) mandate with which they were charged. Yet they seemed not a whit disturbed by what, for all that they themselves had to say to the contrary, appears to have been their expensive and total failure actually to prevent any specifiable and determinate evils.

8.16 Instead—with some sideswipes against certain notoriously callous and uncaring conservatives suspected of contemplating what to all these people would be cruel cuts in both their program and, indirectly, their individual budgets—some of them now proposed, with no awkward self-questioning about past failures, so to reinterpret the expressions "mental disease," "mental disorder," and "mental retardation," as to facilitate demands for (yet more) further funding and extra staff. This and this alone, they suggest, will enable another and more ambitious kind of good to be done, albeit with equally little reason offered for believing that they will have any more success in attaining these different, though no doubt equally worthy, objectives.

8.17 In the perspective of this chapter the most revealing, as well as the most scandalous, feature of the entire *Annual Review* was the form taken by a solitary statement of the need for some systematic monitoring of success and failure. Except for this rare moment of illumination all the contributors were inclined blindly to identify (their) stated intentions with (their) actual achievements. Nowhere in this *Annual Review* was there so much as a hint that systematic monitoring of actual success or failure is essential to the doing of a decent and progressively improving job. Instead the sole reference to this task points in a different direction. A trio of contributors made what at least up to the time of their writing had proved to be, from the standpoint of the "community mental health movement in the United States," an unwarrantably pessimistic statement. This from their point of view unwarrantably pessimistic statement was to the effect that: "[I]t is our strong conviction that prevention proponents will lose the political battle for funding without good data—capable of documenting the effectiveness and social utility of prevention programs" (Price et al., pp. 7 and 288).

8.18 Another example is perhaps rather less vividly scandalous. But partly for that reason it is perhaps more impressively instructive. This is the example of what in the United Kingdom is called not the public but the (state) maintained school system. From its first establishment the pupils in this peculiar publicly owned and managed industry have never been subjected to any comprehensive system of independently assessed examinations. The system has therefore never been able or required to provide any direct measures of the quantity and quality of its output of pupil learning. The only official check on the activities of the schools of which this system is composed has traditionally been the sending in of teams of Her or, as the case might be, His Majesty's Inspectors of Schools. The schools were warned of forthcoming inspections. And in the nature of the case inspectors were able to inspect not the product but only the process of teaching.

8.19 If some state-owned industry charged with the production of some sort of material goods had been managed in this way and if the facts of its extraordinarily hands-off management had become public knowledge, then there is no doubt but that all politicians opposed to whatever was the current administration would have seized on these facts as a heaven-sent example of that administration's almost unbelievable incompetence and untrustworthiness.

8.20 Since the United Kingdom maintained school system is effectively a monopoly, which has for almost the whole of the present century been catering for over 90 percent of all U.K. children, the basic facts about what has been its traditional form of management have always been public knowledge. I say "effectively a monopoly" because any antimonopoly laws anywhere in the world would surely be enacted well before any single supplier won over 90 percent of the market. And this would be so even before taking into account that this particular supplier, being a public service, has always operated what in the ordinary commercial world would have been accounted a policy of predatory notpricing against its independent competitors. I say its "traditional form of management" because in 1988 an Educational Reform Act did at last launch a radical reform program that should eventually result in the construction of the fully comprehensive system of examinations that has so long and so significantly been lacking. But what is so remarkable about the period before 1988 is what did not happen.

8.21 For what is here both so remarkable and for us so impressive is that, regardless of which of the two parties of government was in office, no opposition politicians ever attacked this failure systematically to measure the actual product of this state-owned industry. Since there were no adequate measures of the product it was scarcely possible to raise questions about productivity or the lack of it. One and all appeared to be agreed that the necessary and sufficient condition of educational improvement was an increase in the teacher/pupil ratio—something which in any other industry would have been construed as presumptive evidence of overpersoning. Of course smaller classes are more agreeable for all concerned and involve less assessment and correction work for their teachers. But the belief that they make for more effective teaching is one of those "demonstrated not by the evidence marshalled to support it, but by the lack of any felt necessity to produce evidence" (Sowell 1986b, p. 60).

8.22 When in 1981—as a first, hesitant, and tentative measure of reform—an act was passed to require schools to publish any results achieved by their pupils in any of the then-available independently assessed examinations, the National Union of Teachers (NUT), by far the largest teachers' union in the United Kingdom, revealingly declared its "total opposition." Almost no one responded to this remarkable and revealing declaration as almost everyone would have responded had a labor union representing the employees in some state-owned and state-managed manufacturing industry declared its total opposition to the publication of the findings of investigations into the quality and quantity of material goods produced by that industry.

8.23 Someone might react to all the propaganda for rationality in the present book by pointing out that the most rational of methods and approaches still provides no sure guarantee of true results, adding perhaps as a parting shot that in any case rationality comprises a lot more than the capacity to discern what does and does not follow from what. This is perfectly true. History records innumerable cases of those who believed what for them it was entirely reasonable to believe, and who nevertheless were mistaken in their beliefs. Nor is there any shortage of instances in which hunches and prejudices have turned out to be right and the contrary conclusions suggested by the best available evidence wrong.

8.24 But though the points urged in this reaction are correct, they do not upset what I am saying. First, they do not bear at all upon the contention, which has just been developed (see paragraphs 8.4–8.19) that there is a "connection between rationality in general and personal integrity" (see paragraph 8.6). Second, fallibility is one of the universal and inescapable fundamentals of the human condition. We have no choices between an option of fallibility and an option of infallibility. It is precisely our fallibility which is the best reason why we must always be open to rational criticism. Third, when and insofar as we are confronted with choices between alternative methods of inquiry, then the final judgment can only be a judgment by results. If the shaman or the soothsayer regularly and reliably comes up with predictions that are discovered to have been right while all the economic and scientific advisers get everything wrong, then it surely becomes rational for the Minister to hire and to trust the former while firing and busting the latter. In at least one sense of "rational" it is paradigmatically rational to be thus guided by experience.

8.25 Yet none of this establishes, or would establish, that we can now, or could then, substitute intuition for evidence, or for argument, or for rational appraisal generally. For the very results by which the Minister and everyone else should judge are the discoveries of truths. So we have to be able to identify results as results—to know, that is, that the putative discoveries really are discoveries of truths—before we can say that any method of inquiry in fact is justified by results. It is here that the demand for rational appraisal arises, and with it the challenge to the sincerity of our dedication to truth. At whatever stage these questions of the justification of belief are in fact tackled, they are always logically fundamental. In terms of two ancient but still serviceable distinctions we may say that the context of justification is logically prior, albeit sometimes historically posterior, to the context of discovery.

8.26 It is because we are concerned not with mere assertion regardless of truth, nor even with mere true belief not known to be true, but with knowledge, that we are and have to be concerned with rational justification. It was with that commitment that Socrates lived and died: "The unexamined life is not to be endured."

Selected Bibliography

NOTE. The list below contains all but, with one exception, only those works mentioned in the text that were first published in the English language during the twentieth century. The works of major thinkers of earlier centuries who are mentioned are, with that exception, available in many editions, both hardcover and paperback. So readers wishing to borrow or to purchase copies are best advised to seek up-to-date information on availability either from their local library or from their local bookstore, as the case may be.

Anscombe, G. E. M. *Collected Philosophical Papers of G. E. M. Anscombe*. Oxford: Blackwell, 1981.

Beckmann, Petr. *The Health Hazards of NOT Going Nuclear*. Boulder, Colo.: Golem Press, 1976.

Berg, Charles. *Deep Analysis*. London: Allen and Unwin, 1946.

Brenan, Gerald. *The Spanish Labyrinth*. Cambridge: Cambridge University Press, 1943.

Buchanan, James M. *Constitutional Economics*. Oxford: Blackwell, 1991.

Buchanan, James M., and Gordon Tullock. *The Calculus of Consent*. Ann Arbor, Mich.: Michigan University Press, 1962.

147

Commoner, Barry. *The Closing Circle: Nature, Man and Technology.* New York: Bantam, 1972.

Conquest, Robert. *The Great Terror.* Revised Edition. London: Primolo, 1992.

Cromer, Alan. *Uncommon Sense: The Heretical Nature of Science.* New York and Oxford: Oxford University Press, 1993.

Dawkins, Richard. *The Blind Watchmaker.* New York and London: Longman, 1986.

————. *The Selfish Gene.* 2d ed. Oxford: Oxford University Press, 1989.

Dennis, Norman. *The Invention of Permanent Poverty.* London: Institute of Economic Affairs, 1997.

D'Israeli, Isaac. *The Quarrels of Authors.* London: John Murray, 1814.

Douglas, Mary, and Aaron Wildavsky. *Risk and Culture: An Essay on the Selection of Technological and Environmental Dangers.* Berkeley, Los Angeles, and London: California University Press, 1983.

Efron, Edith. *The Apocalyptics: How Environmental Politics Controls What We Know about Cancer.* New York: Simon and Shuster, 1984.

Epstein, Richard A. *Forbidden Grounds: The Case against Employment Discrimination Laws.* Cambridge, Mass.: Harvard University Press, 1992.

Evans-Pritchard, E. E. *Witchcraft, Oracles and Magic among the Azande.* Oxford: Oxford University Press, 1937.

Flew, Antony. *The Politics of Procrustes: Contradictions of Enforced Equality.* London: Temple Smith; Amherst, N.Y.: Prometheus Books, 1981.

————. *God: A Critical Enquiry.* La Salle, Ill.: Open Court, 1984.

————. *An Introduction to Western Philosophy: Ideas and Argument from Plato to Popper.* Revised Edition. London: Thames and Hudson, 1989.

————. *Atheistic Humanism.* Amherst, N.Y.: Prometheus Books, 1993.

————. *Thinking about Social Thinking.* Amherst, N.Y: Prometheus Books, 1995.

————. *Darwinian Evolution.* New Edition. New Brunswick, N.J., and London: Transaction Publishers, 1997.

Flew, Antony, and A. C. MacIntyre, eds. *New Essays in Philosophical Theology.* London: SCM Press, 1955.

Flew, Antony, and Godfrey Vesey. *Agency and Necessity.* Oxford: Blackwell, 1987.

Goldberg, Steven. *Why Men Rule: A Theory of Male Dominance.* Chicago and La Salle, Ill.: Open Court, 1993.

Gosse, Edmund. *Father and Son.* London: Heineman, 1907.

Hare, Richard M. *The Language of Morals.* Oxford: Clarendon, 1952.

Hills, John, et al. *The Joseph Rowntree Foundation Inquiry into Income and Wealth.* York: Joseph Rowntree Foundation, 1995.

Hume, David. *Essays: Moral, Political and Literary.* Edited by E. F. Miller. Indianapolis, Ind.: Liberty Classics, 1985.

Huxley, Aldous. *Eyeless in Gaza.* London: Chatto and Windus, 1936.

Huxley, Julian. *Essays of a Biologist.* London: Cape, 1923.

Levin, Michael. *Feminism and Freedom.* New Brunswick, N.J.: Transaction Publishers, 1987.

Luttwak, Edward. *Coup d'Etat: A Practical Handbook.* Baltimore and Harmondsworth: Penguin, 1969.

Magee, Bryan. *Popper.* London: Fontana, 1973.

Marx, Karl, and Friedrich Engels. *The Holy Family.* First published in German in 1845. Translated by Richard Dixon and Clemens Dutt in *The Collected Works of Marx and Engels.* Vol. 4. New York: International Publishers; London: Lawrence and Wishart, 1932 onward.

Morris, Desmond. *The Naked Ape.* London: Corgi, 1968.

———. *The Human Zoo.* London: Cape, 1970.

Murray, Charles. *Losing Ground: American Social Policy 1950–1980.* New York: Basic Books, 1984.

Orwell, George. *1984.* London: Secker and Warburg, 1949.

———. *The Collected Essays, Journalism and Letters of George Orwell.* London: Secker and Warburg, 1968.

Popper, Sir Karl. *The Logic of Scientific Discovery.* London and New York: Hutchinson, 1959.

———. *Conjectures and Refutations.* London: Routledge and Kegan Paul, 1963.

———. *Objective Knowledge: An Evolutionary Approach.* Oxford: Clarendon, 1972.

Price, R. H., R. F. Ketterer, B. C. Bader, and H. Monahan, eds. *Preven-

tion in Mental Health: Research, Policy and Practice. Beverly Hills and London: Sage, 1980.

Rawls, John. *A Theory of Justice.* Cambridge, Mass.: Harvard University Press, 1971.

Richardson, Ken, and David Spears. *Race, Culture and Intelligence.* Baltimore and Harmondsworth: Penguin, 1972.

Rockwell, Joan. *Fact in Fiction: The Use of Literature in the Systematic Study of Society.* London: Routledge and Kegan Paul, 1974.

Rolt, L. T. C. *Isambard Kingdom Brunel.* London: Longmans Green, 1957.

Ryle, Gilbert. *The Concept of Mind.* New York and London: Hutchison, 1949.

Schneider, F., and C. Gullans, eds. *Last Letters from Stalingrad.* Toronto: Signet, 1965.

Schopenhauer, Arthur. *The Art of Controversy.* Translated and edited by T. B. Saunders. London: Sonnenschein, 1896.

Silberman, Charles E. *Criminal Violence, Criminal Justice.* New York: Random House, 1978.

Smart, Ninian. *The Religious Experience of Mankind.* London: Fontana, 1971.

Sowell, Thomas. *Civil Rights: Rhetoric or Reality?* New York: William Morrow, 1984.

———. *Knowledge and Decisions.* New York: Basic Books, 1986a.

———. *Education: Assumptions versus History.* Stanford, Calif.: Hoover Institution, 1986b.

———. *Compassion versus Guilt and Other Essays.* New York: William Morrow, 1987.

———. *Is Reality Optional?* Stanford, Calif.: Hoover Institution, 1993.

Stephen, H. J. *New Commentaries on the Laws of England.* 21st ed. Vol. 4. London: Butterworth, 1950.

Stevenson, C. L. *Ethics and Language.* New Haven, Conn.: Yale University Press, 1944.

Thurow, Lester C. *Poverty and Discrimination.* Washington, D.C.: Brookings Institution, 1969.

Trevor-Roper, H. R. "The European Witch Craze of the Sixteenth and Seventeenth Centuries." In *Religion, the Reformation and Social*

Change. London and Toronto: Macmillan, 1956. This long essay was later published separately by Penguin, 1969.

Urban, W. R. *Beyond Realism and Idealism.* London: Allen and Unwin, 1949.

Veblen, Thorstein. *The Theory of the Leisure Class.* New York and London: Macmillan, 1899.

Warren, Earl. *The Memoirs of Earl Warren.* New York: Doubleday, 1977.

Wilson, James Q. *Thinking about Crime.* New York: Basic Books, 1975.

Wilson, James Q., and Richard J. Herrnstein. *Crime and Human Nature.* New York: Simon and Schuster, 1985.

Wittgenstein, Ludwig. *Tractatus Logico-Philosophicus.* Translated by C. K. Ogden. London: Kegan Paul, Trench, Trubner and Co., 1922.

Index of Personal Names

Anscombe, G. E. M.: 4.8
Aquinas, St. Thomas: 1.25
Aristotle: 1.32–1.33, 2.15, 3.27, 5.38, 6.51, 7.25–7.26
Augustine, St. of Hippo: 5.29

Bacon, Francis: 2.10
Baldwin, James: 3.2
Beckmann, Petr: 6.9
Berg, Charles: 4.28–4.29
Boswell, James: 5.27
Brenan, Gerald: 6.7
Buchanan, James M.: 4.16
Buchanan, President James: 1.39
Burke, Edmund: 1.36, 7.22

Cantor, Georg: 1.45
Carmichael, Stokely: 3.2–3.3, 3.8
Carroll, Lewis: 5.32, 7.3
Castro, Fidel: 3.2, 3.8

Index of Ideas

The purpose of this index is to provide a checklist of the various ideas and distinctions systematically explained and employed in the text above, a checklist which makes it easy for readers wishing to do so to test themselves and/or to refresh their memories. It therefore makes no attempt to include every notion which makes an appearance in the text.